"Matthew Schwartz is one of the great TV news investigative reporters in America over the last twenty-five years. This book is riveting and a must read."

—MORT MEISNER, TV news agent

"Matthew Schwartz is a reporter's reporter—a top-notch investigative journalist in the tradition of Edward R. Murrow and Mike Wallace. For decades Matthew hasn't been afraid to tell it like it is, even when his personal safety has been threatened standing up for the public's right to be informed. From interviewing serial killer 'Son of Sam' to dodging a swinging baseball bat wielded by a maniacal gypsy, Matthew has been a pugnacious fighter—a fighter for the truth. Now in his absorbing debut memoir, *Confessions of an Investigative Reporter,* you can savor the 'inside' stories behind his reports in a remarkable four-decade career.

"I worked alongside Matthew at WOR and WWOR-TV, and although we were often rivals, we respected each other and I admired his honesty and thoroughness as an investigative reporter. He's engaged in public brawls with disreputable salesman and confronted con men and dirty detectives—his stories are responsible for putting them away in jail.

"Matthew's reports on homeowners scammed by unlicensed contractors even got his viewers to donate their time to resolve their predicaments. He's covered four New York mayors and risked his health reporting on 9/11 from Ground Zero. His compelling memoir is a must-read for journalism aficionados and anyone interested in finding out the risks and hardships involved in getting the 'real story.'"

—CHARLES GOMEZ, author, *Cuban Son Rising*; former correspondent, CBS News and NBC News

"Matthew Schwartz is my kind of reporter. We are both old school. Matthew believes in the most important tenets of investigative reporting: do the research, do the legwork, know all the facts, and go after the bad guy!

"When we were competitors in Tampa, whenever one of Matthew's stories came on one of the many monitors we had in the newsroom of the competition, I always turned up the sound and knew I was going to see a story I wished I had uncovered.

"Although investigative reporting is in my mind the best job in journalism, it is not easy. It involves long hours, reams of paperwork to go through, endless phone calls, meetings with victims and whistleblowers, getting more info on the story with the hope that some will talk on camera. Matthew never shied away from doing that work in order to button up all the angles of the story. He was also tenacious and fearless in tracking down the bad guy to hold him or her accountable.

"I'm also aware of the great work he did on obtaining an exclusive interview with 'Son of Sam' serial killer, David Berkowitz. While that interview occurred before Matthew came to Tampa, I'm aware of it and the work he put in to make that spectacular piece happen.

"Matthew is also an excellent storyteller, and if you have any interest in the behind the scenes of a top-notch investigative reporter, I know you will want to read his book.

"I've seen a preview of some of the book and I guarantee it is a page turner that you will have a tough time putting down.

"During my six-decade career in broadcasting, I've worked with and against some talented investigative reporters. Matthew Schwartz is among the top tier of those I've encountered in my career."

—MIKE DEESON, former investigative reporter, WTSP-TV, Tampa/St. Petersburg, Florida

"Matthew Schwartz propels us into a world few of us have seen or even imagined with this candid behind-the-scenes memoir of his years as a prominent investigative reporter. The stories he shares have impacted lives and often changed them for the better.

His honesty, his ability to be self-deprecating alongside being duly proud of his accomplishments, and his page-turning words all spin together to make this a rocketing must-read book!"

—LALA CORRIERE, best-selling author

"Congratulations to my valued colleague and friend, on forty-plus years of success, working in the toughest trenches of a very rough TV news business!

"You survived, you thrived, and now you get to share with us the quirky, captivating, and compelling details behind the stories that fueled excitement in newsrooms, and filled millions of TV screens all those years.

"Matthew never let go of the full passion, focus, and doggedness that have been his arsenal for exposing wrongdoers. You see it in every story he produces. And you'll read about it on these pages."

—TOM MCNAMARA, former anchor, KVOA-TV, Tucson

"Matthew Schwartz is the scourge of scoundrels because he digs and digs until he gets the goods on the crooks that prey on ordinary people. Hidden cameras, undercover stings, sifting mountains of documents from the coroner, stakeouts, confrontational interviews—whatever it takes. In 10,000 stories over decades, he chased down a judge, nailed a pill mill over-prescriber, a scam school operator, a towing racket, the movers from hell, and a whole colorful catalogue of outrageous rascals.

"Viewers and readers benefit from Matthew's New York hustle, weapons-grade chutzpah, relentless work ethic, and massive experience. Matthew and I have been friends and colleagues since a previous century when we had our first television reporting jobs in a small town. I've always enjoyed (and learned stuff) from his exploits."

—JIM RANDLE, former Beijing Bureau chief, Pentagon correspondent, anchor, and editor at Voice of America

"After four decades in television news, a few former colleagues truly stand out. Matthew Schwartz is one of them. Matt is the real deal! We have known each other since the late 1970s when we worked together at the ABC affiliate in Richmond, Virginia.

"As it happens, we are both graduates of Ohio University in Athens, which has one of the top broadcast journalism programs in the country. The foundation laid for us as undergraduates served us well as we pursued our television news careers. Matthew is among the smartest, most gifted journalists I have ever known. He has always approached his craft with a sense of fairness and a relentless pursuit of the truth.

"In an era of journalistic self-aggrandizement, Matthew is a definite exception. As you will read in the following pages, Matthew has never made himself more important than the story he is telling. I could not offer any higher praise!"

—FRANK ROBERTSON, former TV news anchor and reporter

"I had the pleasure of working with Matthew at WWOR-TV for several years back in the day when television was BIG. Matthew cared a great deal about his work and it showed.

"He had the guts that it takes to be a top-notch investigative reporter. Believe me, there was tons to investigate in the number one television market in America.

"When you love what you do it shows. Read his book. Guarantee you will like it."

—LLOYD LINDSAY YOUNG, former weatherman, WWOR-TV, New York

"I first met Matthew in 1994 when I went to work for WWOR-TV. I soon learned why he had earned the reputation he had as a member of one of the best investigative teams in the New York market.

"Fast forward to 2013, and the station I am working for, KVOA, is looking for an investigative reporter to launch its new franchise. I told my news director, 'If you can get Matthew Schwartz, he's all you'll need.' He did not disappoint, quickly earning the nickname 'Freight Train' as the investigative reporter who rolled into town taking down evildoers and anyone else who dared to take advantage of the residents of our city.

"From an exclusive interview in New York with the 'Son of Sam' killer, David Berkowitz, to bringing down a corrupt moving business in Tucson and the thousands of stories in between, Matthew has had an incredible career spanning four decades. Now we finally get to hear the stories behind the stories."

—SEAN MOONEY, anchor and reporter, KVOA-TV, Tucson, Arizona

"Matthew Schwartz has been a close friend since we shared workspace and room and board while cutting our journalistic teeth at the ABC affiliate in Richmond, Virginia, in the early '80s. Matt went on to a distinguished career as an investigative reporter in, among other places, the nation's premier TV market of New York City. The streets there yielded a treasure of fascinating stories, including an exclusive interview with Son of Sam serial killer David Berkowitz. Fair, tenacious, and untiring in his pursuit of the truth, Matt presented finely crafted tales of some of the most interesting stories of our lifetime. The details of the tales that didn't always make it to air will be an enjoyable and interesting read to curl up with on a cold rainy night. Matt is a unique colleague and one I am proud to call a friend."

—JIM BAILEY, longtime TV news director, anchor and reporter

Confessions of an Investigative Reporter

by Matthew Schwartz

© Copyright 2020 Matthew Schwartz

ISBN 978-1-64663-073-8

*REVIEW COPY: This is an advanced printing subject
to corrections and revisions.*

Published by

 köehlerbooks™

210 60th Street
Virginia Beach, VA 23451
800-435-4811
www.koehlerbooks.com

To Dave,

I hope you turn out top-notch reporters.

April 2020

Matt [signature]

confessions
of an INVESTIGATIVE
REPORTER

MATTHEW SCHWARTZ

VIRGINIA BEACH
CAPE CHARLES

For Michael, Jason, and Jessica.

Now you know what your old man really did for a living.

And for every investigative reporter who courageously holds the

powerful accountable and gives voice to the voiceless.

"To be persuasive, we must be believable.
To be believable, we must be credible.
To be credible, we must be truthful."

—EDWARD R. MURROW

"We got the bubble-headed bleach-blonde who comes on at five
She can tell you 'bout the plane crash with a gleam in her eye
It's interesting when people die
Give us dirty laundry."

—DON HENLEY

AUTHOR'S NOTE

The quotes from those investigated and all interviewees are exactly as they aired on television. They were taken from scripts and tapes, not from memory. Charges or allegations are supported by and taken from police, court, and other official records.

TABLE of CONTENTS

FOREWORD

For the more than three decades I've known Matthew Schwartz, he's been a reporter from the old school—the same one I came up in, modeled after the dusty Chicago news bureau slogan "If your mother says she loves you, check it out."

In New York, where I worked alongside him, and later in Tucson where I often visited friends and sources during my own long career at NBC News, I watched Matt do the work the good ones do: gathering the evidence and, when it added up and only then, chasing down the bad guys to demand an explanation. His targets were the usual rogues gallery: doctors whose over-prescribed oxycodone and methadone prescriptions killed patients instead of helping them; con men (and women) pushing phony security guard certificates or nonexistent services; corrupt judges and politicians; unrepentant killers.

Matt spent decades in that corner of journalism often called *investigative reporting.* In my own half-century career, in print and on TV, I always thought that term was either overused or redundant, because in my view a reporter's work should by definition involve varying levels of *investigation*. It's not enough to hear a good yarn and pass it along. To have any value and credibility, assertions must be tested, measured and corroborated, and ultimately accepted or rejected solely based on the facts gathered along the way.

That may seem a quaint and even pointless notion in our post-factual digital age and social media fog, but in fact it's never been more important to find voices worthy of trust. Matt, an admittedly imperfect human being who nevertheless had a perfect understanding of journalism's best uses, was one of those voices.

Matt's best guess is that in his long career he had a byline on around 10,000 reports for seven stations across the country. A lot of those reports were the standard "if it bleeds, it leads" assignments— the arson fires and drunk-driving smashups, and homicides that are the pulse and punctuation of local TV news. But Matt found his wheelhouse and made it his signature: deeply reported pieces that often ran five to seven minutes, or longer—an eternity in the typical newscast. They were stories he found himself rather than hearing about them from the assignment desk after a review of the day's papers (and now websites); stories he *enterprised* and then investigated with the ultimate goal of informing his viewers at the very least, and, in his best results, helping them if he could.

In his long reporter's journey, Matt's genuine curiosity about the world around him often drew him towards stories that could only be nailed down through exceptional patience and a sharp understanding of why those specific stories would resonate with his viewers. He was, as he saw it, an everyman, and if a story interested him, it would surely interest his audience.

When David Berkowitz, the Son of Sam killer who shot six women to death over a several-months siege of terror in the mid-'70s, was weeks away from a parole hearing, it was Matt who landed the exclusive one-hour interview. It was a classic *get*, an interview sure to appeal to anyone still fascinated or repulsed by Berkowitz's almost mythical explosion of violence.

And it was Matt who told the wrenching story of a dying 6'10" addict and denizen of an urban drug den who decades earlier had been a can't-miss high school hoops phenom—a phenom exploited by coaches and hangers-on and abandoned as soon as he lost his grip on the glittering potential and terrifying threats that buffeted him until he broke.

I've had my own reporter's byline since my mid-teens, and along the way I've learned a few things about our breed. First and foremost, we're human, with all that implies. Matt uses the word *confessions* in his book title and doesn't sugarcoat his own shortcomings and bleak moments of personal history.

The thing is, Matt kept at it year after year and decade after decade because of a single truth that is universal in our chosen craft. And finding the next great story remained the failsafe response to everything, including a faltering relationship, worries over money, a dented self-confidence, the punishing office ecosystem. That was Matt's gift—the ability and the willingness, no matter what else was happening in his life, to find that story and structure it for television in ways that assured maximum impact.

What I've liked best about Matt's work is that he never settled for the on-camera gotcha, the low-hanging fruit you knew was coming in every report. He first gave you the context, the background, the documentation—the unglamorous but essential elements in any report that mattered. That's why you could trust Matt's reporting; I did and still do.

And now, if you want the backstory behind so many of the reports of his that generated their own headlines or moved the chains towards justice or redemption, you can dive into *Confessions of an Investigative Reporter.*

Check it out!

**Mike Taibbi, former correspondent,
NBC News, December 2019**

INTRODUCTION

I sat next to a serial killer. A berserk gypsy swung a baseball bat at my head. I was caught in the middle of a full-scale brawl at a public meeting. I was shoved and spit on by sleazy salesmen. I was arrested for trespassing on the property of a moving company I investigated after receiving dozens of complaints about its business practices.

I did numerous reports on people later sent to prison or jail. Among them were two online con artists, a dirty detective, a mom who gave her baby away, and a big-time college basketball coach. Following my series about dogs and cats dying in airplane cargo holds, President Clinton signed a law making air travel safer for pets. Dozens of my stories on homeowners scammed by unlicensed contractors prompted viewers to donate time and money to fix the problems. Those stories drove some scammers out of business.

All of this drama—and so much more—occurred while I was a television news reporter from 1977 to 2020. I worked at seven stations in six cities: Utica, New York, from 1977 to 1979; two stations in Richmond, Virginia, from 1979 to 1981; Cleveland, Ohio,

1

1981 to 1983; New York City, 1983 to 2003; Tampa, Florida, 2005 to 2009; Tucson, Arizona, 2013 to 2020.

Nearly half my career was at one station in the New York market. I covered four mayors, four trials of mob boss John Gotti, and the tribulations of countless more law-abiding folks. I covered 9/11 from Ground Zero and did a half dozen interviews with a bombastic real estate developer who, in 2016, became America's president.

Although I won some awards and lasted twenty years in the biggest market in the country, I did not have the best on-camera presence. I had a nasally voice, a New York accent and a weight problem during my last twenty-five years on TV.

However, I worked hard and was consistent over a long run, like major league pitcher Don Sutton. In twenty-three seasons, he won twenty games only once. He was never what's called "tenure dominant." But Sutton is in the Hall of Fame for his steady excellence.

My job was to inform viewers by exposing bad actors or practices. That was my goal when deciding to be a reporter while a junior in high school. TV journalism would also allow me to make a decent living while having fun. I would become a survivor in a competitive business driven by ratings and strong personalities.

I saw solid reporters get fired simply because new bosses wanted reporters they had worked with previously. I saw reporters quit before they reached age fifty due to burnout or job frustrations. They wanted less stressful jobs with better hours. We were expected to be news machines. During my run, I told approximately 10,000 stories. But there were hundreds more I couldn't tell.

Some weren't politically correct enough for management. Others were deemed inappropriate or irrelevant. And many stories weren't told simply due to the time constraints of local news. Finally, many of those gems that were spiked now have a home in these pages.

My passion for championing right and exposing wrong came from my mother. Shirley Schwartz fought for underdogs and the little guy her entire life. Mom hated bigotry and prejudice. I began to learn this when I was seven years old, and the little guy was me.

I had been called a "dirty Jew" by an older, bigger kid on two occasions while riding my bicycle past his house on the way to the candy store. This was in River Edge, New Jersey, a wonderful, sleepy suburb about twenty miles from midtown Manhattan. My family moved there from the Bensonhurst section of Brooklyn in 1955, when I was two.

I didn't know the name-caller. He went to the private Catholic school in town, and I went to the public elementary school.

After the second verbal assault, I came home in tears. I was also angry. I was thinking I'd punch the kid in the face if it happened again. I tried to hide my tears from my mother. She asked what was wrong, and I reluctantly told her. She asked for the boy's address, which I withheld. I was afraid she'd go there and make a scene and then the bully would seek me out and beat me up as retribution.

Mom wouldn't stop asking for the address. She said, "His parents need to know what he called you, so they can educate him on prejudice." I didn't fully understand the meaning of the word, but after several minutes of Mom persisting, I capitulated. The last digit of his address was barely out of my mouth by the time Mom was out the door.

After she told the boy's mother about the name-calling, I never had a problem with him again. When I went to the store, I could have taken a different street and avoided his house. But Mom had given me the courage to pass his home. I didn't look at him or taunt him in any way; I was just ready to fight if I had to defend myself. Even if I got pummeled.

My mother dragged me to civil rights rallies when I was young and would rather be playing sports. She had me read books about civil rights and civil injustices, about Sacco and Vanzetti and stories with David vs. Goliath themes.

She was married to a Navy officer during World War II and was pregnant when she received a telegram from the Department of Defense informing her that his ship was bombed. He was missing and presumed dead. That was the government's way of telling war wives they were widows. It was seven years before she met the man who became my father. She had put herself through school and became a registered nurse. She later raised four children while my dad worked long hours selling insurance.

Dad's schedule prevented him from attending some of my Little League Baseball games, and his baseball knowledge was average at best. So, I was surprised when the other fathers nominated him to become league president before one season. I soon saw why. The league had been trying unsuccessfully for years to get a business to sponsor a scoreboard. By opening day, we had a beauty, thanks to Dad persuading Pepsi-Cola to pay for it. I think I inherited some of my father's sales skills, which came in handy during difficult story assignments.

After my siblings and I started school, Mom became well known for her handmade stained-glass windows and lamps, and ceramic trays. Some of her pieces decorated buildings in northern New Jersey, and she taught those crafts in local adult education programs.

Years later when Mom was diagnosed with diabetes, she studied the disease and became a diabetes counselor. During the Yom Kippur War in 1973, when she was nearing fifty, she volunteered to serve as an Israeli Army nurse and served for three weeks there. When she died at the age of eighty-five in 2009, she was buried in her Israeli Army uniform. I was chosen to give the eulogy.

I focused on her toughness and empathy, traits that became engrained in me along with her righteousness. Mom gave me a sense of purpose, and by age fifteen I knew my destiny would be to become a reporter, to tell stories, to entertain and to inform.

I had majored in journalism at Ohio University and loved everything about the classes and the campus in Athens. I worked on the university's radio station and newspaper. That's where I became involved in a controversy on campus. It was my first big story. Once I got the "bite," it never went away.

During my senior year at OU in 1976, three of my housemates were football players, including a co-captain. Ed Madison was a six-foot-three, 250-pound offensive lineman. Off the field Ed was a sweetheart, a big teddy bear, which made the story I would write more difficult.

I received a tip that some football players were smoking weed on the team bus en route to away games. I was a sports reporter and columnist at the college paper, *The Post*. It was highly regarded and unusual among college papers then because it was published every weekday, not once a week like many others, and averaged sixteen pages a day.

I co-wrote the story about the pot-smoking players with our sports editor. The piece was picked up by the Associated Press and widely reported in Midwest newspapers. Some big papers even mentioned my name, which was heady stuff for a twenty-one-year-old. Journalism professors at OU praised it in their classes as a solid example of investigative reporting. The football players, not so much. Including my roommates.

The story ran in the spring, and I had to live with the three football players for two months until graduation. Talk about awkward. They ignored me. Walking around campus, I was nervous and looked over my shoulder. I only went to classes, the radio station, and the newspaper office. I stayed away from bars and parties. I was afraid some football players would use me as a tackling dummy. Even when there were parties in the large house we lived in, I remained in my bedroom in the back.

Days before graduation, I asked Ed if I could talk to him about the story. I explained why I had to write it. I told him it was so wrong for college athletes, most of whom were getting a free ride on their education, to be getting high riding to games. I told Ed we had different agendas, that as an aspiring journalist, I couldn't ignore the story. As an aside and as a friend, I told him since he was a co-captain and knew about the pot smoking, he should have told his teammates to stop it. Ed said he understood my position, and our friendship was restored. Like so many of the stories in the years to come, I never made it personal.

Although I worked in several cities, the bulk of the earliest years of my career were in the nation's largest TV market.

Like many in broadcast journalism, my goal had always been to be a TV reporter in the Big Apple. But I had to pay my professional dues first. My earliest on-camera job was in Utica, New York, the country's 154th TV market out of 212. I worked there for twenty-two months and it felt like five years. Another professional hop landed me in Richmond, Virginia. I liked Richmond, but it was the country's fifty-fourth market. I wasn't there long either, having been recruited to Cleveland, the ninth largest. It would be the stepping-stone I needed to land my dream job in New York.

It was tough telling the WWBT Richmond news director I was leaving after only three months. I was nervous walking into his office and thought he might tell me to leave immediately. He was disappointed, but said since I didn't have a contract, there was nothing he could do. I started working in Cleveland three weeks later.

My salary jumped from $17,500 a year in Richmond to $28,000. That wasn't a bad salary in 1981. I was twenty-seven, single, and had no debt. Working in Cleveland also gave me the chance to reconnect with some friends and fellow alumni of Ohio University. And WEWS had a great history. It was the first commercially licensed station in Ohio and sixteenth-oldest station in the country.

During my two years in Cleveland, my on-air name was "Matthew Shaw." When I was hired, I told the news director I'd like to use "Shaw." My father called himself "Mel Shaw" when he played violin in a band when he was young due to anti-Semitism. His real name was Murray Schwartz. (As Don Rickles would say, "Jewish? I took a guess.") I liked the sound of "Matthew Shaw" but later felt like a hypocrite. I wasn't very religious but felt I was trying to hide being Jewish. When I was hired in New York, where I had many friends from high school and elsewhere, I went back to using my real name.

My jump to New York started with a call from my mother.

"Your father has cancer and has six months to live."

I immediately called my agent and told him to go all-out in getting me a New York job so I could be near my father. I always wanted to work there, and now I needed to. I needed to spend time with Dad during his final days. He lived seven months after I got the job and was so proud to see me on TV.

My dream was to work in New York by my thirtieth birthday. My first day of work in New York was exactly on my thirtieth birthday. I was one of two nightside reporters and would do a live shot most nights. I eventually became tired of doing ninety-second stories that would be quickly forgotten, like day-old newspaper lining puppy crates. I'd work on a story for hours, and at least once a week the assignment editor would call with breaking news. The story my photographer and I had been doing would be dropped to fifteen or twenty seconds with an anchor voice-over. I would report live from the scene of breaking news, often arriving minutes before the newscast. Sometimes I had no choice but to use a line I came to despise: "Details are sketchy, but police say . . ." After a while I refused to use the word "sketchy" and instead said something like, "This just happened and investigators are sorting out the specifics." I often tried to get a live interview with an eyewitness or first responder.

This run-and-gun journalism was stressful, and the hours often kept me away from home, even on holidays.

On Christmas night 1989 I was in an editing room as my editor finished my story for the 10 o'clock news. I was about to go home to my wife and two infant sons.

An assignment manager came into the room and said Yankees manager Billy Martin had been killed in a truck accident near his home in Binghamton, New York. It was three hours away. He said I needed to head straight up there.

My photographer and I were greeted by a blizzard in Binghamton. A cop told us Martin's pickup truck was at a nearby garage. We were surprised to see the vehicle out in the open and not surrounded by crime tape. I had never experienced the ability to get so close to a vehicle involved in a fatal wreck. Especially since there was an investigation pending into whether Martin's friend, who was driving and survived, was drunk (he was convicted of drunken driving).

The garage was closed and the photographer and I got close enough to touch the wrecked vehicle. To this day I can still see a grisly sight: strands of human hair, stuck to cracks on the passenger side of the shattered windshield. This was how I spent part of the holiday season. Three hours from home, in a snowstorm, looking at a dead man's hair. Probably Billy Martin's hair.

I didn't use any tight shots of it. Too morbid.

After nine years on the job at WWOR, I was feeling burnt out. I started thinking of getting a job in public relations, what's known among journalists as "moving to the dark side." But on April 1, 1992, the news boss, Tom Petner, called me into his office.

"I'm beefing up the investigative unit and adding you to it," Tom said. I had been hoping for this for years. It was the chance to do more substantive and longer stories that could make a difference in people's lives. No more covering "crime de jour," as reporters called murders, rapes, robberies, and fires, on a nightly basis. Instead of doing quick stories five nights a week, I would do one report a week that could run anywhere between five and seven minutes. Occasionally I would do a same-day piece with an investigative angle on the day's biggest story. I would have a producer to help with research. I felt rejuvenated.

Being an investigative reporter would define my career. I broke several big stories that went national or had huge impact. Among them was interviewing serial killer David Berkowitz.

PART I

New York
Confessions

1983–2003

CHAPTER ONE

The Son of Sam and Fake News

"If I'm at a wedding and they play 'Daddy's Little Girl,' I get up and walk out of the hall."

—MIKE LAURIA, whose daughter was murdered by David Berkowitz

O ne of the most notorious killers in history was sitting three feet from me. David Berkowitz, the self-proclaimed "Son of Sam," the ".44 Caliber Killer," had murdered six people and wounded seven others in a shooting spree that terrorized New Yorkers over thirteen months in 1976 and 1977. Berkowitz targeted attractive young women, most with long brown hair. Many who fit those descriptions had dyed their hair blonde and cut it short to avoid being noticed by the target of the biggest police manhunt in the city's history.

Decades later, the serial killer and I became pen pals.

In the spring of 2002, I was an investigative reporter at WWOR-TV, Channel 9. The station moved in 1986 from Times Square, where it had different owners and the call letters WOR-TV, to Secaucus, New Jersey. The town was six miles from midtown Manhattan and known for decades as the home of pig farms and the odors they emitted. But I loved working there and had wonderful, talented colleagues. WOR-TV was also a superstation, meaning it was on cable systems nationwide, which made my mother in Florida happy. Despite the move to New Jersey, the station remained in the New York City market, the largest TV market in the country.

Berkowitz's home was seventy miles north, in the Shawangunk Correctional Facility, a maximum-security prison in Upstate New York's Sullivan County.

Berkowitz had a parole hearing approaching, and I thought he might want to talk about it. The hearing was a legality, a requirement for inmates having served twenty-five years. There was no chance of him being paroled; he had been sentenced to six consecutive terms of twenty-five years to life.

Berkowitz became my pen pal after my producer, Ethan Dreilinger, went to the prison without a camera and visited him. The killer requested the meeting before agreeing to the interview. Ethan did a great job laying the groundwork, assuring Berkowitz that our piece would not be sensational. Little did I know about one sentence that would be added to the story. But without Ethan's help I doubt Berkowitz would have done the interview.

Berkowitz and I then exchanged letters for about six weeks. The former letter sorter with the United States Postal Service wrote that he agreed to talk to me before the parole hearing in July 2002. He wanted the public, especially the victims' loved ones, to know that he realized he deserved to stay in prison. Like so many inmates,

Berkowitz claimed he found religion behind bars and was a Jew for Jesus. He wanted to tell the world he had changed. He had sent a letter to New York governor George Pataki, saying, "In all honesty, I believe that I deserve to be in prison for the rest of my life. I have, with God's help, long ago come to terms with my situation and I have accepted my punishment."

This interview was a great *get,* as it's called in the news business.

His birth name was Richard Falco. He was given up for adoption because his father was a married man who threatened to end his affair with Berkowitz's mother if she kept the baby. Berkowitz was adopted by Nathan and Pearl Berkowitz. He was traumatized by Pearl's death in 1967, and became a loner.

Berkowitz was arrested, ironically, due to a run-of-the-mill parking ticket. A woman was walking her dog in Brooklyn shortly after 2 a.m. on July 31, 1977, near the scene of one of his shootings. She told police she saw cops giving out tickets nearby. Investigators then reviewed all the tickets handed out in that area during the time of the murder. One of the tickets was issued to a David Berkowitz of Yonkers, New York. New York City cops called Yonkers police and spoke to an officer who knew Berkowitz as a local "cuckoo, a nut." Berkowitz had no police record, but as detectives interviewed his neighbors, they became strongly suspicious.

Cops staked out Berkowitz's apartment building. He was arrested as he sat at the wheel of his car on August 10. He has been quoted as telling police, "I guess this is the end of the trail," and "How come it took you so long?" and "You got me." Later that night, when police paraded him from a precinct station to court with dozens of cameras and reporters present, he smiled. He was twenty-four years old and getting attention for the first time in his life. He appeared to like it.

Twenty-five years later I was in a prison interview room waiting for Berkowitz. I had two photographers with me for one of the few times in my career, in case of technical problems and for cutaways (reverse shots of me). There would be no second chance.

I wasn't nervous. I felt some pressure to ask every question I thought he needed to answer. Although I had several pages of questions, as I routinely did for major interviews, I would deviate from them if he said anything that needed a follow-up question.

Berkowitz smiled as he entered the room. I stood to greet him and extended my hand. People have asked me how it felt to shake hands with a serial killer. *Weird.* I thought about what he did when he held a gun in his hands. I didn't want to shake his but felt I had to. Refusing to do so would not get the interview off to a good start.

Berkowitz said in a soft, high-pitched voice with a New York accent, "OK, nice to meet you." He was forty-eight years old but could have passed for sixty. Prison can do that. He was pudgy, graying, balding, and wore glasses. I could find dozens of guys on the outside who resembled him, except for the three-inch scar on the left side of his neck. He was stabbed by an inmate trying to make a name for himself at Attica State Prison in 1979.

I started the interview by asking, "When you lie in bed at night, what do you think about?"

He said, "It's not easy sometimes, when the lights go out and the door slams shut every evening, to reconcile things and come to terms with things. But I think I've come a long way."

I brought old newspapers with articles about the murders. I started to hand them to him, but he didn't take them and barely looked at them. He said he hadn't read a newspaper since he'd been behind bars. It was clear he was uncomfortable seeing those headlines.

Berkowitz said he was teaching inmates about God and the Bible. He was in a video recorded in prison, calling himself not the "Son of Sam" but the "Son of Hope." He would have talked about that the entire time if I let him; he gave longer answers about religion than anything else.

He apologized to his victims' families and friends, but did not want to talk specifically about the murders or why he committed them. Even so, I asked repeatedly.

Berkowitz had done very few interviews over the years, and I thought viewers would want to know his motivations. His initial confession to cops was that he was commanded to kill by voices he heard from a black Labrador retriever owned by his neighbor Sam Carr. Hence his self-given nickname. Berkowitz told me, "It was a time of torment for me, a time of chaos when these things happened. My feelings on parole are that I've accepted responsibility for what has happened. I'm doing my time in prison and I'm not trying to get out of prison."

Berkowitz claimed he was in a drug-induced haze when he committed the murders, and he said he didn't remember clearly why he killed. "I'm sorry for what happened," he said. "I'd do anything if I could go back and change it."

I had no intention of making the piece a pity party for Berkowitz, so I interviewed the parents of two women he killed. Donna Lauria was his first victim. The pretty eighteen-year-old student and her girlfriend Jody Valenti had been at a disco on July 28, 1976. As Jody told police, shortly after 1 a.m. the women were in Jody's car discussing their night out. They were in front of the Bronx apartment building where Donna lived with her parents. Berkowitz walked up and fired four gunshots through the passenger window. Donna was shot in the neck and died instantly. Jody survived.

I asked Mike Lauria what he would do if he ever was face-to-face with his daughter's killer. In his thick New York accent, he said, "My hands would be on his t'roat and I'd rip it outta his neck. That's da hatred I have for this man." I wanted to hug the guy; I felt such pain for him. I showed Mike a letter Berkowitz had sent me claiming he found religion.

"If he found God, then he'd better come to me, because I'm da pope," Mike said. "I don't believe him. I don't believe anything he says. The hole that this man has left in my heart, nobody has any idea, unless you walk in our shoes."

I also interviewed a legendary NYPD detective named Joe

Coffey. He had taken Berkowitz's confession. We did the interview at the scene of one of Berkowitz's murders in Queens. Coffey thought Berkowitz was a scam artist, and his claims that he wanted to stay in prison were about self-preservation. Coffey said, "I think he realizes, coming out here, somebody's gonna take a shot at him."

Coffey was known by reporters for giving colorful sound bites, and he didn't disappoint. Recalling Berkowitz's confession, Coffey said, "For three hours he didn't blink his eyes once. He had a constant smile on his face, and it was like talking to a zucchini. It was like going to the vegetables section of the supermarket and looking at his face." It was the only time I heard a serial killer, or any other criminal, compared to a zucchini. But I knew what Coffey meant and thought viewers would, too. Berkowitz was stoic and vacant. It was a great, telling soundbite.

Most of my interviews were under ten minutes because I usually had enough good sound bites within that time. But the Berkowitz get was obviously a special one with a lot of ground to cover. It ran about an hour and fifteen minutes.

I felt good about the interview, which was odd for me. I was always hard on myself. In my entire career there were fewer than ten stories I wouldn't change a thing about. I always reflected on something I could have done better.

When I returned to the station, some news managers wanted to see the raw footage. This was less than two years after Fox bought the station, and I thought the news writing had become sensational, tabloid style.

But I never thought that would include lying.

While watching the footage, the news director noticed my pen was on the table between Berkowitz and me. He said, "Weren't you nervous about your pen being between you and Berkowitz? You should say something about being nervous about Berkowitz picking up your pen and stabbing you with it."

I was stunned. *Murder by Bic?*

I wasn't sure I heard him correctly, and if I did, *he must be joking*, I thought. But he was serious. I was being asked to lie. The other two news managers in the room said nothing. They were good journalists and nice guys, but I think they didn't want to disagree with their boss.

This was *fake news,* years before the term became popular. I wasn't nervous about the pen on the table. In fact, the thought of being attacked with it never entered my mind. Two corrections officers were in the interview room. A high-ranking prison official told me earlier the born-again Berkowitz was "a model inmate, a teddy bear." He wasn't going to stab a reporter on camera. It also wasn't relevant and would make part of the story about me. It wasn't that I was being old school. I was trying to provide viewers with insight into a serial killer's mind.

I explained this to the news director and said I would not mention the pen. He frowned, shrugged and shook his head. He was not happy. Nor was I. I left the managers' meeting after watching the footage thinking, "Son of Sam my ass. Son of a bitch."

Before the meeting I was excited about what the interview meant for the station. I'm competitive, and Channel 9 was in a constant ratings battle with the other two stations that had 10 p.m. newscasts, Channels 5 and 11. That month was a ratings period. The ratings months were February, May, July, and November, and they determined how much stations charged for commercials. I despised ratings, called "sweeps" in the business. Some news directors I've worked for implied if not told talent that we needed to do our best work during ratings. Anchors and reporters were not allowed to take vacations in ratings months.

I always tried to make every story the best it could be regardless of when it aired. The stress levels of many news managers increased noticeably just before and during ratings. I thought that was a lousy way to live.

In May 2002, none of the other New York stations had an interview as big as the Son of Sam. Our station would heavily promote it and it would air after our highest-rated program, which was, believe it or not, one of those fake "professional" wrestling shows.

I spent two days transcribing the interview and writing the piece. I left out the line about the pen and liked the script I brought to management.

The news director who wanted me to say, "I was nervous about Berkowitz picking up the pen and stabbing me with it," changed it to this: "My producer made sure that my pen was out of the killer's reach."

My producer, Dreilinger, wasn't even at the interview!

He told me in 2019 that he also wasn't in the office that day. He was off because his wife was pregnant and not feeling well. Also in 2019, I asked the other two news managers if they remembered the news director's directive. One didn't respond; the other said he didn't remember it. To me, the person whose name and face were out there, it's as clear as yesterday. And my producer recalled the story and being off that day.

That line still pains me now when I watch the piece.

Of course, I made mistakes in forty-four years of reporting. But they were unintentional. This was the only time I knowingly told a lie on television. I was infuriated. I would have quit but couldn't afford to, with three young kids and a big mortgage.

The Berkowitz report was eight minutes and four seconds long. It was the longest piece I did on Channel 9. There were so many good exchanges between Berkowitz and me I could easily have gone longer. Management decided to run about three and a half additional minutes of the interview at 10:30 p.m., teasing viewers throughout the newscast's first half hour that "there's more to come."

There was more to come for me, and it wasn't good. The Son of Sam report, a highlight of my career, led to my downfall at the station.

You can watch the Berkowitz interview on Vimeo at https://vimeo.com/344179853.

In August, three months after the Berkowitz piece, the assistant news director called me and said the station's general manager wanted to see me in his New York office later that week. I had never been summoned by the GM. My contract was up September 30, and I knew the new news director was not going to renew it. Especially since the Berkowitz story.

I worked hard at my profession. I knew how to cultivate sources, which often led to hard-to-get interviews or other stories. Also, I was meticulous with my facts and would not get a station sued, despite aggressive stories. The only two lawsuits filed against me were dismissed when the bad guys' lawyers saw all the proof I had on their clients. It isn't rocket science to say that television station owners, like those in other businesses, care primarily about two things:

1) Making money.

2) Not getting sued.

They also care about doing good things in the community, but that comes in a distant third—no matter what any TV station owner or executive will tell you. I walked into that meeting knowing great stories and not getting sued wasn't enough to save me.

The GM got to the point immediately. "We have decided to go in a different direction and we're not renewing your contract," he said. This was the ambiguous and standard management line that to me really meant "We think you suck, are too old, and make too much money."

I was also told that instead of keeping me until the end of my contract only five weeks later, they would let me finish out the year, which was decent of them. At the end of the five-minute meeting, I stood, and the GM shook my hand.

I think the new Fox management believed I was too old school for its type of sensational journalism. Plus, I was just shy of fifty and making $174,500, and they could hire reporters at half my age and half my salary.

In fairness to Fox, I must admit I wasn't completely blameless for my firing. I had gained a lot of weight over the years. Appearances matter in television news. Stresses at home and work had ganged up on me. They did not, however, affect the quality of my reports.

I had a hectic work schedule with long hours that I tried to balance with family life. I coached my kids' sports teams while trying to keep up with the Joneses in my upscale town. I leased a Mercedes with a $676 monthly payment. I had an addition put on the house that cost $120,000 and wasn't necessary. I built up a large credit card debt, and despite my salary wasn't saving.

Worst of all, I did something I always vowed I never would: I got a toupee. My father went bald in his mid-forties, and at age forty-five, I was worried I'd be bald soon.

Within minutes of showing up in the newsroom for the first time with it on, an assignment editor asked me, "Did you do something to your hair?" A friend told me that radio star Howard Stern, while complimenting a report I did, mentioned my hairpiece on his show. Two years later I threw it in the trash. I now call my midlife crisis "toupee and too fat."

Getting fat, going bald and refusing to sensationalize and lie on camera ended my run at WWOR, but not my future or my life. New opportunities would arise elsewhere to find and tell stories again.

It's ironic: My biggest get in New York helped to get me.

CHAPTER TWO

All-American Tragedy

S O U N D   B I T E

**"No way would he be the person
you are talking about."**

—New York Police Department lieutenant Robert McKenna,
after being told a drug addict he arrested many times was a
former all-American basketball player.

L es Cason was an all-american high school basketball player in the early 1970s. He was six feet, ten inches with skills ahead of his time for a big man. He was a terrific outside shooter with a sweet jump shot and handled the ball like a point guard. Cason led East Rutherford High School to New Jersey state championships in 1971 and 1972. He scored 2,871 career points, then the most in Bergen County boys basketball history, and fifth all-time in the state. And this was before the three-point shot came into existence. His coach was Dick Vitale, who later gained fame as a broadcaster. Cason received 320 college scholarship offers. I was a big basketball fan but never went to watch another school's game—until I went to one of Cason's.

Cason went to Rutgers University, and Vitale road his coattails to land a job as an assistant coach at the New Jersey school. Cason had two undistinguished seasons at Rutgers. He played harder off the court and flunked out. He attended a junior college in Texas and dropped out. Then he seemingly vanished, which is hard to do for a person that size. He hadn't been heard from or written about in fifteen years. Some of his high school friends and teammates thought he might be dead.

In October 1987, Allen Levine, a producer and writer at WWOR, called me while he was on vacation. He said, "Did you read Newfield's piece today in the *Post*?" Jack Newfield was a great investigative reporter and had written about recidivist drug offenders in New York's Washington Square Park. The place in lower Manhattan was a haven for drug dealers and users. Cops kept arresting them and judges kept releasing them because the jails were overcrowded. One guy was mentioned in the column only as "Les," and there was a small mug shot of him. He had been arrested nearly 100 times. He was described as "a tall, thin African-American." Levine grew up near me in Bergen County and like me followed high school basketball. He too knew of the mystery of Les Cason, so we decided to pursue our instincts together.

I called the Manhattan district attorney's office and asked the public information officer two questions: "How tall is this 'Les' guy you've prosecuted so often, and how old is he?" I knew that since Cason graduated from high school in 1972, he would be thirty-two or thirty-three.

"He's six foot ten and thirty-three," the PIO answered.

"It's him," I told Levine.

I got a photographer and we went to Washington Square Park to look for a lost legend.

We met a New York City Police Department lieutenant at the park named Robert McKenna. He was thirty-six years old and straight from central casting: six feet tall with a sturdy build, handsome with jet black hair and sky-blue eyes. (I wasn't surprised when years later he retired and got steady work as an extra on the TV cop drama *Blue Bloods*.)

McKenna had arrested Les dozens of times for dealing drugs. I showed him photos of Cason from his high school yearbook. He said the guy we were looking for looked like the teenager in the photos but had lost a lot of weight and many teeth. He said he was a drug addict and dealer who went by "Slim," and "William Davis." The cop asked me why I was so interested in Cason.

"I'll tell you when you're on camera."

I used this technique on certain stories when interviewees were okay with it because I learned that their answers would be more spontaneous. When I told McKenna about Cason's basketball stardom, his shoulders slumped and he almost staggered. He took a step back and said, "You're kidding, right?" I wanted spontaneity and I got it big-time. After the interview I took McKenna to our news van and showed him old game film of Cason. He couldn't believe it was the same person and several times shook his head in sadness.

The photographer and I walked the park for two days looking for Cason with no luck.

On day three, we spotted him. He was indeed emaciated and missing a lot of teeth. Leaving the photographer far away because I didn't want to anger or scare Cason, I walked up to him, politely introduced myself and told him I saw him play in high school and remembered his amazing career. He testily said, "Sir, you keep calling me Les. My name is not Les." It was incredibly sad.

I told Cason that a lot of friends and fans were worried about him; they didn't know if he was dead or alive. He exited the park and I did not follow.

I brought the video to the home of Cason's mother, Mary Johnson. She confirmed it was him and said she knew he was a drug addict. She was heartbroken but said she was not surprised. She was one of the few people he kept in touch with and said he would only visit East Rutherford after dark because he was ashamed of what he had become. She said Les didn't want to be seen in the town where he was still remembered as a star. She agreed to an interview and said, "I've tried to get him help, but he can't stop." We also showed the video to a couple of Cason's old friends and high school teammates. They had trouble believing this was indeed him.

I spoke on the phone with Vitale. He lived in Florida and my station wasn't about to spend the money to fly me there, and this was before FaceTime or Skype. Regardless, I had a strong sense he didn't want to talk about this on camera even if my station hired a Florida crew. Vitale had received criticism over the years for using Cason in his career climb to become a college coach. I asked Vitale if he took any responsibility for letting Cason play with his poor grades and partying while in high school. He said only that the Cason saga was "one of the saddest, most disappointing things in my career."

After the report aired, I received dozens of calls from viewers. Many thanked me and said they often wondered what happened to Cason. Despite Cason's condition, some viewers were grateful knowing he was alive and hoped he would seek help. Most gratifyingly, I was asked by several schools to visit classrooms and show students the report. Teachers, administrators and coaches wanted kids, especially athletes, to see what can happen when you don't apply yourself academically and do drugs. When my report was shown in classrooms and I was able to be there, I always studied the expressions on the students' faces. Many shook their heads in sadness. I heard some students say, "Oh my God."

On the Sunday after the piece aired, *The Record*, the big newspaper in Bergen County which extensively covered Cason in high school, led its sports section with our story.

Ten years later, in April 1997, I was on vacation with my family in Disney World when a WWOR assignment editor called. Les Cason had died of complications from AIDS. His life ended in a nursing home in Harlem. He was forty-three years old.

Lieutenant McKenna told me Cason wanted to see him, the cop who arrested him so often, and asked the nursing home to call him in his final hours. McKenna visited him and later said Cason weighed fifty pounds. He said Cason broke down crying and expressed sadness for how he ruined his life.

His old coach, Vitale, reportedly paid for the funeral.

CHAPTER THREE

Dying to Fly

SOUND BITE

"He's passed out, he's not conscious and he's covered with feces and urine and vomit."

—Donna Calk, on her golden retriever's condition after the dog was
in an airplane's cargo hold during a cross-country flight

The Channel 9 I-Team Received several complaints in 1998 from viewers who were heartbroken. Their pets died or were injured while in airplane cargo holds. I thought the airlines needed to be held accountable.

One call came from a New Jersey woman named Donna Calk. She and her family had flown from New York to California. Their beloved golden retriever, Jed, just twenty-one months old, was in the plane's cargo hold.

After the family landed at Los Angeles International Airport, they found Jed in a back room. The dog was clearly in distress. "By the time we got to the veterinary clinic in west LA, he was not breathing," Donna told us. "And that was it."

28

The vet said Jed died of hypoxia—suffocation due to lack of oxygen.

A woman named Roberta Eldridge had flown with her cat, Gabi, from New York to Tulsa. After the plane arrived and Roberta retrieved Gabi, she recalled, "I looked down at her, and she took a last meow. And she just died. I couldn't believe it. I thought I was in a nightmare."

The vet said the cat died of a heart attack. She had been exposed to near zero-degree temperatures in the airplane's cargo hold.

These were not isolated cases. We found that every major US airline had been accused of violating the Animal Welfare Act. Under the law, pets could not be exposed to temperatures of more than eighty-five degrees or less than forty-five degrees for more than forty-five minutes. The Air Transport Association said a half million pets fly every year, and that "only" 5,000 turn up dead, injured, or missing.

Our early research was so disturbing, the story so multi-layered, it led to an investigation that we worked on for the next six months.

We needed to see the conditions for pets on planes firsthand. So my producer Allison Gilbert went on a flight with a healthy five-year-old poodle–cocker spaniel mix named Abu. With his owner's permission, Allison attached temperature and humidity sensors to the roof of the pet carrier holding Abu. They flew on Continental Airlines from Houston to Miami.

At both airports, Abu's crate was left sitting on the hot tarmac. Although shade was inches away, no one on the cargo crew moved the crate.

When Allison took the indicators out in Houston, they showed Abu had been exposed to 115-degree heat and 80 percent humidity. She noticed bleeding in his groin and rushed him to a veterinarian. The vet said, "It took a good bump in that area to cause that much bleeding." The dog's carrier had apparently banged into something during the flight, meaning that either the crate or the contents around it were not adequately secured.

We wanted to find out how many more cases there were like Abu's. We called every major airline and requested their records on pets and safety.

Not one airline provided records.

They said they didn't keep those statistics and that they didn't have to. The federal government didn't require it. The only numbers available were from the Air Transport Association, a trade group that represented the airlines. Not exactly an unbiased group. Pet travel was and still is regulated by the Department of Agriculture. An agent with that agency named Ron DeHaven told us, "If we would be able to identify a problem, whether it is industry wide or with a particular airline, I can see real value in having those numbers."

We ended the taped portion of the piece with a memorable sound bite from Roger Caras. He was an animal activist who became a network correspondent with ABC and president of the American Society for the Prevention of Cruelty to Animals.

"There's not enough oversight," Caras said. "And I'll tell you, animals are not cargo. Cargo can't hurt. Cargo does not feel. Cargo can't be afraid. It's inert. Animals can be frightened, they can be fried, they can be frozen, they can be dropped. They can be forgotten."

At the end of the piece I reminded viewers that the Department of Agriculture could only regulate; it couldn't enact laws. That of course would be up to Congress.

The promotions department titled the story "Dying to Fly," and it aired on November 3, 1998. I liked the title and the eventual results.

Soon after "Dying to Fly" aired, we were bombarded with calls from viewers who said their pets were injured during flights. One of the calls was the kind that reminded me again why I loved doing this work. It came from an aide to then New Jersey senator Frank Lautenberg. The staff member said Lautenberg saw the story and was so disturbed by it that he planned to talk to colleagues about sponsoring legislation that would make air travel safer for pets. I told the senator's aide I needed Lautenberg to say that on camera, and he did in a follow-up piece.

On April 5, 2000, President Clinton signed the "Safe Air Travel for Animals Act." It required airlines for the first time to report monthly to the US Transportation secretary on the loss, injury, or death of passenger pets. The data would be published so consumers could find out an airline's record on pet safety.

In other words, airlines would now be held accountable. This was one of the most gratifying end results of any story I ever did.

Lautenberg's staff issued a release which said, "Senator Lautenberg introduced the pets-on-planes legislation after viewing a report by the WWOR-TV UPN 9 News I-Team, which exposed the lack of regulations and detailed the bad experiences consumers had when they transported their pets by commercial airlines."

This was the best resolution possible. We aired an investigation that resulted in a new, tougher law. It is one of the stories I am most proud of. Not only as a reporter, but as a dog lover.

Another result of the story, much less important, involved a call I received from a producer with the Montel Williams show asking me to appear on the program. I had been asked before to do local radio to plug an upcoming piece or discuss one that aired the night before. I always declined unless instructed to appear by my boss, which happened only a couple of times. I figured my stories should speak for themselves. And we had a promotions department to spread the word. But my news director wanted me to do the Williams show thinking it would be good publicity for the station. The program was syndicated nationally on dozens of stations. I also thought it would be fun.

I did the show and it went well. A clip of "Dying to Fly" was shown. When the studio audience saw the part about the young golden retriever that died, I heard gasps. After the report's ending sound bite, the beautifully articulated line from Roget Caras, I saw people in the audience wiping away tears.

I donated the $350 I received for appearing on the show to a pet shelter.

CHAPTER FOUR

Security School Scam

SOUND BITE

"Why are you running, Gene? Why are you running? I want to ask you a few questions."

—Me, trying to interview the owner of a security guard school

A couple of young, unemployed men who lived in Brooklyn were angry when they called me in 2002. Felix Santiago and Ramel Anthony wanted jobs as security guards. They said they went to the Smith Institute on lower Broadway in Manhattan to take an eight-hour class. The training was required to obtain a state-stamped certificate to work as a security guard.

The men said when they showed up at the training school, the owner, Eugene Smith, told them they could get a certificate by simply paying him twenty dollars. They claimed Smith said no training was necessary. They both forked over twenty bucks.

They later went to a security company that was hiring guards to work at buildings around the city. The manager asked them about the training they received at Smith Institute. Felix and Ramel told the manager they received no training. The security company manager said he couldn't hire anyone without the eight-hour course.

The certificates the young men bought were worthless. And they were still unemployed.

After I got off the phone with the young men, I researched state regulations on certified security guards and confirmed what they told me regarding the mandated training. I then interviewed Felix and Ramel, along with managers at two security guard companies.

Rather than just confront Smith about the young men's claims, I wanted his scam caught on camera. I had a colleague go to the Smith Institute with an undercover camera.

I was excited when my colleague called me with details of what happened at the undercover shoot. I was more excited when I saw the video. It showed the Channel 9 employee walking into Smith's classroom. Two young guys who were real applicants were also there. One of them told Smith, "We want to be security guards." Smith said, "You wanna get a certificate? Let's see, you need one piece of ID and I'll give you a certificate."

The photographer told Smith he had left his ID at home (he didn't want Smith knowing his name and home address). Smith responded, "No problem." He put a certificate into his typewriter and began filling in the blanks. The paper said our photographer had "successfully completed the eight-hour course." In the report I said, "Eight-hour course? He was there about eight minutes!"

After Smith handed over the useless paper, my undercover colleague said something to Smith that made me laugh: "It's easier than what I thought." Smith then continued to make the story better. He said, "As long as you have a high school diploma, make a nice appearance, you'll do fine in security. You just gotta pay me $25." Since Felix and Ramel had told me they paid Smith $20, he raised his rate.

After our photographer handed over the cash, Smith told him, "You'll do fine in security." After that sound bite, I said, "He'll do fine in security? He didn't have a minute of training!"

The day after the undercover shoot, I went to the Smith Institute. My photographer and I saw him alone in the classroom, but the door was locked. We waited in the hallway out of his sight for more than an hour.

Smith came out of a back office to the hallway. With the camera rolling, I said, "Hi, Mr. Smith, I'm Matthew Schwartz from the Channel 9 I-team." Smith looked at me, then looked at the camera, clearly stunned. He looked up at the elevator next to the three of us. We were on the fifth floor. He obviously didn't want to wait, so he started running down the stairs. Nothing like running away from a reporter if you want to appear guilty. He apparently knew we were onto his scam.

I shouted, "Why are you running, Gene? Why are you running? I want to ask you a few questions." He said nothing as we ran down to the lobby. He ran outside and lost us on the crowded sidewalk. But we had more than enough.

After the story aired, I received at least a dozen calls from viewers who said they too paid Smith $20 or $25 for certificates and couldn't get hired by security firms. Like a lot of scam victims I've talked to over the years, they complained to me but not the investigating agencies. Another call I received came from an investigator with the New York State Division of Criminal Justice. He wanted the phone numbers for the victims so he could interview them.

A couple of months later, the state announced it was not renewing its approval of the Smith Institute, and the school shut down.

CHAPTER FIVE

Corrupt Car Dealership

SOUND BITE

"The dealership is selling used cars and telling buyers they're new."

—A tip from a mechanic who worked at the dealership

I received hundreds of complaints about car dealerships. The most common came from buyers who said they bought a lemon, or the dealership changed the finance terms after the sales papers were signed. I've reported on two dealerships that sold vehicles with salvage titles. They were in a wreck or a flood and the dealership didn't disclose that as required by law.

My favorite investigation about a car dealer came in the late '90s. It began with a phone tip that was the best type of tip—an employee who saw the illegal stuff going down. He was a mechanic at a dealership in Union County, New Jersey. He claimed the shop was rolling back the mileage on odometers and selling the cars as new. I'd heard of this before but never got proof.

A few days later the mechanic did an interview with me with his face digitized and voice muffled. This was unusual because employees were understandably afraid of getting fired if they talked to reporters, even if unidentified. The mechanic told me after the piece aired that the dealership investigated to find the tipster; it never found out. The place was breaking the law, cheating customers, but was more concerned with who talked to me about it. They wanted to fire the messenger.

The mechanic said he saw the odometer rollbacks done on a weekly basis. He claimed the dealership's owner and some managers were driving new cars home *for up to a year.* Then, when the boss wanted to put those cars up for sale, an outside mechanic would show up and roll back the odometers from as many as 10,000 miles to single digits. They would detail these cars, add new tires if needed, and put them in the new car showroom.

We decided to follow the general manager from his Bergen County, New Jersey, home to the dealership, a thirty-three-mile trip. Channel 9 rented a van for us that had the name of a phony dry-cleaning business on it and dark-tinted windows. For three days I drove while my photographer, Scott Salem, got video of the guy leaving his house and driving to the dealership. A few days later, our tipster called to say the car the GM had been driving was being prepped for sale. This was what we were waiting for.

My photographer went inside the dealership to pose as an interested buyer while I stayed in our van a few blocks away. Scott was wearing a baseball cap containing a hidden camera. He got behind the wheel and focused his "cap camera" on the odometer. It read *000007.0* Seven miles. It would not be a lucky number for the GM or his business.

I later confronted the GM in his office, camera rolling. He turned red and kicked us out, yelling while walking through the showroom as customers stared. He said, "You're wrong. You don't know what you're talking about." I asked, "How am I wrong? We have video of you driving that car about 200 miles." He just kept saying, "Get out."

Prosecutors didn't think I was wrong. They charged the dealership with consumer fraud. The GM unfortunately had a heart attack around that time. He survived, but his dealership did not. Seems not many people wanted to buy "new" cars there anymore.

About ten years later I did a story on a Tampa car dealership selling vehicles that had been flooded in a hurricane. They did not disclose that the cars had a salvage title. The dealership was charged with consumer fraud by the attorney general and eventually closed.

CHAPTER SIX

Real and Fake Brawls

"So much for public meetings."

—An angry woman after a brawl broke out at a county freeholders meeting

A ll reporters cover public meetings when residents tell elected officials, "Not in my backyard." We call it "NIMBY." A phone company wants to put a cell tower in their neighborhood, or a fast-food company wants to build on their block, or Walmart wants to open a store. I experienced this firsthand at its most vitriolic in 1987 while covering a meeting in the northwest New Jersey town of Newton.

The Sussex County Board of Chosen Freeholders was considering where to put the county's garbage when the landfills were full. Shortly after the call to order, everything went out of order.

The small meeting room was packed with angry residents of Lafayette Township, which was the likely location for the dump. Several women brought infants in strollers to the meeting. It began with residents screaming at board members about not being heard. Sensing the audience's anger just minutes in, the board chair said, "We are taking a recess." All hell broke loose. The residents did not want the discussion to continue in executive session. They wanted to be heard publicly and immediately.

Some spectators rushed the freeholders' table when the recess was announced. People were screaming, strollers were overturned, babies were crying. I saw a mom pick her baby up out of a stroller, then throw the empty stroller at the supervisors' table. I was relieved the mom removed the baby first.

Residents blocked the door so freeholders couldn't go into a private meeting. Punches were thrown by people on both sides. The board chairman landed a solid right on a citizen's jaw. The chairman then got shoved to the floor by a couple of audience members. Photographer Roy Isen, Micki Sellers doing audio, and I stood in the middle of everything. Roy kept panning around because so much was going on, and he didn't miss a highlight. It's not easy to keep your cool while having a blind side due to the camera. And in those days the cameras were much bigger than they are now. I always stood on the photographer's blind side. No one was seriously hurt before sheriff's deputies came to restore order.

When I got back to the station and the producer saw the video, it became our lead story on that night's newscast. I was live on the set and wrote this for my lead-in: "There's an old saying that you can't fight city hall, but today a lot of people fought *in* city hall."

I ended the taped part of my report with a sound bite from a homeowner who yelled, "So much for public meetings" while the freeholders were in recess. An ironic, funny line. Our video was requested by the *CBS Evening News with Dan Rather*, which ran it the next night. Almost the entire piece consisted of footage of the fight.

It was a reminder to never go into a story with a preconceived notion of what will happen. Never expect a meeting to be boring, especially if it's about where to put a garbage dump.

Around that same time in the mid-'80s, some people who watched professional wrestling still thought it was real. This was before World Wrestling Federation boss Vince McMahon finally came out and acknowledged that pro wrestling is "entertainment." His pronouncement surprised only the young and the naïve.

Pro wrestling had big ratings on our station and others around the country. I admit to occasionally watching. I got a kick out of some of the characters, especially George "The Animal" Steele, "Captain" Lou Albano and "Sergeant" Slaughter. Their overacting cracked me up.

I also noticed a few wrestlers getting sloppy in their fakery, such as talking to each other in the ring not so subtly when close together. That gave me an idea. This wasn't Watergate, and it wouldn't win a Pulitzer, but it could be fun.

Photographer Paul Tsakos and I arrived at the Meadowlands Arena in East Rutherford, New Jersey, hours before the night's matches. I had Paul put a shotgun, or "boom" microphone, under the wrestling mat. During an American Wrestling Association match between Larry Zbyszko and Bob Backlund, our mic clearly picked up the two of them planning their next move.

The conversation between Zbyszko and Backlund went like something this:

> **Zbyszko:** "OK, I'm going to throw you across the ring. I'll lie down in the middle. You bounce off the ropes and go to jump on me. I'll roll, and you land face first."
>
> **Backlund:** "Got it. I'll sell it."

I somehow convinced the owner and promoter of the AWA, the former wrestler Verne Gagne, to come to our studio to watch the footage. After seeing it two or three times, I asked what the wrestlers were discussing. Gagne said, "Not knowing . . . [long pause here] exactly what they are talking about, it's hard for me to say. But I see how you could think they were planning their next move." The subject wasn't serious enough for me to press Gagne, so I just smiled and let the audio speak for itself.

The story created a buzz because it may have been the first time anything like it was so clearly caught on camera. It was maybe the best proof for even the believers that pro wrestling was fake. Its fans didn't care; its ratings remained strong.

What wasn't funny a few years later was the number of wrestlers dying young after abusing steroids and other drugs.

CHAPTER SEVEN

Celebrity Encounters of the Weird Kind

SOUND BITE:

"Matt, mind if a light up a doobie? I'll share it with you."

—Dizzy Gillespie, legendary trumpet player

My first job after college was at WCBS News Radio 88 in New York City. I was hired two weeks after graduating mainly because I had a connection. The morning drive co-anchor, Jim Donnelly, was a neighbor of mine in New Jersey. Donnelly was one of Dad's insurance clients. I had no idea Donnelly was on the radio until my father told me when I was seventeen; I listened only to the music stations (except during Mets games). I began to listen to WCBS and found it exciting. I got a rush from breaking news and appreciated how smooth the anchors and reporters were while broadcasting live with so much going on around them.

While home on break from college during my junior and senior years, I went to Jim's house several times at 2:30 a.m. to ride with him to WCBS to observe him and the staff at work. Jim was on the air from 5 a.m. to 9 a.m. I got to know the process and the bosses. By the time I graduated, the top managers knew me. I had called the manager of news operations periodically during my senior year to remind him I would be graduating and wanted badly to work at WCBS.

Days after graduation, the news manager called me in for an interview. When I arrived, I saw a two-foot-high pile of resumes on his secretary's desk. I saw mine on top and felt optimistic. A half hour later, I was hired for an entry level job. I would be a "desk assistant" in title, a gopher by responsibilities. I was overjoyed. I took the elevator down from the newsroom on the sixteenth floor of the famous midtown Manhattan building known as Black Rock. But it felt like I was floating out of there.

I would be working in the Big Apple alongside big New York names. Among the street reporters: Art Athens, Irene Cornell, Jane Tillman Irving, Jerry Nachman, and Steve Reed. The anchors included Lou Adler (Donnelly's co-anchor), Ben Farnsworth, Harvey Hauptmann, Ralph Howard and Gary Maurer. The movie critic was Jeffrey Lyons. The sports director, Ed Ingles; the sports reporter, Spencer Ross. They had voices I could die for. I was intimidated to be in their presence. But they all were so friendly and helpful to this twenty-two-year-old rookie who asked a lot of questions. Howard, the midday anchor, also lived in my town and drove me to work when I had the 7 a.m. to 3 p.m. shift because he had press license plates and could park in special zones near the station.

When I switched over to television a year later, and for the rest of my career, I often tried to help an intern or production assistant. I would approach them in the newsroom and ask what their goals were. I would let them go on shoots and shadow me. That was in part because of the kindness I was shown during my first job.

It felt surreal when my first paycheck from WCBS Radio arrived because it contained the big, black-and-white CBS logo, the so-called "Eye," the same logo on the paychecks of Edward R. Murrow (the greatest and most important broadcast journalist ever), Walter Cronkite and other iconic broadcasters.

I didn't care that the check for my first two weeks' pay was about $600.

One morning in January 1977, seven months after I was hired at WCBS, word reached the newsroom that Bernard "Toots" Shor had died at the age of seventy-three after an undisclosed illness. "Toots" was supposedly coined by an aunt when he was a toddler. Only close friends knew his real name. He owned a legendary New York restaurant he preferred to call a saloon. Many people called it America's most famous bar because of who hung out there. Toots's customers included hundreds of athletes, politicians, mobsters, and show-business stars. Among the latter was Jackie Gleason. "The Great One" was a regular and one of Toots's closest friends.

Shor's death was announced on a slow news morning, and the station needed content. Adler was on the air and he was also the news director. When he heard about Shor's death, he said, "Can we get a friend of Shor's on the air?" I told Adler during a commercial break that my uncle knew Gleason, lived near him in Florida, and I could try to get Gleason on. I knew it was a long shot, but I was trying to move up the ladder. I had nowhere to go but up. In retrospect I should have told the managing editor instead of Adler. Then, in case I failed, maybe Adler wouldn't find out and be disappointed. When I told him my idea, he said, "Go for it."

I called my uncle, who was a marginal celebrity himself. My father's younger brother was Irving Fields, a fantastic pianist well known in New York and South Florida. Uncle Irv and his trio recorded several albums and had a couple of hits he composed, the most famous being a 1946 number called "Miami Beach Rhumba." He played in numerous New York restaurants, piano bars, and on cruise ships. Irv was 101 years old when he died in 2018. He played right up to his final days.

I asked Irv for Gleason's phone number. He called Gleason and told him about Shor's death and asked if it was okay to give it to me. Gleason agreed, and minutes later I was so nervous that I was shaking as I dialed Gleason's number. I had never called anyone as famous. Also, I was a huge fan of his, having been addicted to *The Honeymooners* for years. (I still watch the "Classic 39" episodes often and laugh out loud at the same lines I've heard hundreds of times.)

Gleason was very polite, especially considering it was about 8 a.m. and he was still a renowned late-night reveler. But I could hear the sadness in his smoky voice as I gave him the few details we knew about Shor's death. I asked if he would pay tribute to his pal on the air during a live interview with our anchors. He agreed. I then panicked over transferring the call correctly. But I figured it out and Gleason proceeded to do a terrific few minutes on the air.

Afterwards, Adler, who rarely talked to desk assistants and was so tough he often scared even veteran reporters, walked up to me, patted me on the back and said, "Good job." That was a high compliment coming from him, and I was thrilled.

About a month later I was promoted to chief desk assistant. It meant I was the chief gopher. I think my pay increased from $300 to $350 a week. I felt fantastic.

Dizzy Gillespie was one of the greatest jazz trumpet players ever. I was excited when he agreed to do an interview with me for a series I was doing in 1985 about the many famous musicians who lived in New Jersey or were born there. This was before I was moved to the WWOR-TV investigative unit. The series was called *Sinatra to Springsteen.*

Dizzy told me on the phone that he had a recording session in New York the day of the interview. The television station was then located in Times Square. Dizzy lived in Englewood, New Jersey, which was on the way from my home to the city. I offered to drive him to the studio, and he accepted. I was happy to be able to spend more time with him. I also thought it would be a good way to prepare for the interview.

When I arrived at Dizzy's home, I saw a huge, gold trumpet on his front lawn; it must have been twenty feet wide. I was somewhat nervous, mostly about potentially getting in an accident because I was so focused on what he had to say.

After crossing the George Washington Bridge, we were on the West Side Highway when Dizzy, then sixty-eight years old, asked me, "Matt, you like the weed?" I said, "Excuse me?" even though I heard him. Dizzy said, "You know . . . reefer. Me and the boys in my band enjoy it."

Musicians getting high was not surprising. I told him I smoked some pot in college but not since. He then asked, "Mind if I light up a doobie? I'll share it with you." Now, that did surprise me, that a famous person whom I'd just met was so candid. Not to mention he was considerate enough to ask if I minded. I was silent for a few seconds, thinking, *This is really awkward.* I didn't want to upset him because I needed this interview. I didn't know if he'd cancel it if I wouldn't let him smoke a joint in my car. I might have taken him up on it if I weren't driving and on work time at my dream job.

I imagined the headlines: *Jazz legend busted, reporter fired.*

I told Dizzy, "I hope you don't mind, but I can't smoke on the job. And I can't take the chance of getting stopped by a cop." He said no problem, he could wait until after the interview. I never considered mentioning this in the report that aired. I thought it would be an invasion of his privacy and irrelevant to the focus of the piece. I told some friends about it after Dizzy died in 1993. I always thought it was a cool story, and that Dizzy Gillespie was one relaxed, cool cat.

I wanted variety in the *Sinatra to Springsteen* series, so I included the Sugarhill Gang. Their 1979 hit "Rapper's Delight" was the first rap single to become a Top 40 hit on the Billboard Hot 100. My photographer and I went to their studio (also in Englewood), and the guys performed "Rapper's Delight" for us. Since they weren't wealthy enough to quit their day jobs, I asked what they did. Henry Jackson, known by his stage name, "Big Bank Hank," worked at a pizzeria. We went there and Hank flipped dough high in the air while singing "Rapper's Delight" on camera. We edited the piece cutting back and forth between Hank on stage in the song's music video and in the pizzeria. It was a fun, creative element in the story. Sadly, Hank died in 2014 at the age of fifty-eight from cancer.

Anthony Benedetto was another Bergen County resident for years. He was better known as Tony Bennett, one of the world's greatest singers.

For many years, my mother taught ceramics and stained glass in an adult education program at a local high school. Bennett's wife was one of her students. One weekend morning when I was about ten, I was playing touch football in front of our house with neighborhood kids. At some point we noticed a guy with dark curly hair standing on the curb watching our game. We had no idea who he was and didn't pay attention to him. I figured he must be the husband of my mom's student and forgot he was there. His wife and my mom were working in our basement, where Mom had her workshop with three kilns of different sizes.

The spectator apparently grew restless, and after about a half hour of watching he went back into our house. I came in soon after our game was over to see the Bennetts leaving. My wonderful father, who was once on the periphery of the music business and fancied himself as a friend of some celebrities, tried to sound hip. As Bennett walked out, my father shook his hand and said, "Take care, T. B."

As soon as the door closed, my mother said to Dad, "You idiot! No one calls him that. And it stands for tuberculosis!" I cracked up, and for years I'd say to Dad, "Take care, T. B."

After the couple left, Mom asked me, "You know who that man is?" When she told me, I shrugged. I didn't realize what a star Tony Bennett was and would be for the next sixty-plus years.

On a chilly, overcast March day around 1990, I was headed with a photographer to the Hamptons on eastern Long Island's South Fork. Known as a summer destination for the affluent, there had recently been a significant decrease in the number of people renting summer homes there. We wanted to report why and what it meant for potential renters and business owners.

On the more-than-two-hour drive from the station to the Hamptons, photographer Todd Fenton told me that the office of the realty agent we were going to interview was across the street from a restaurant that Billy Joel frequented. Todd was a big fan of Joel's, and so was I. Todd said, "How cool would it be to interview the 'Piano Man'?" I agreed it would jazz up a piece that I worried might be dry. I also knew it was extremely unlikely we would run into Joel during a dreary afternoon in the off-season.

We arrived early for the interview with the agent, so I asked Todd to get video of the marina and other establishing shots about a mile away. He dropped me off at the realty office so I could do the pre-interview. The office was on a main road, so I briefly stood outside and took notes of the names of some of the businesses for possible interviews later.

I was there maybe two minutes when I saw a man get out of a large, silver Mercedes. It was Billy Joel.

I immediately called Todd and told him to rush back because I was going to ask Joel for an interview and didn't expect him to wait, if he even agreed. Todd thought I was joking, but I assured him I wasn't. Joel was walking directly towards me, on his way to the restaurant Todd had mentioned. He was alone, no bodyguard or entourage. That only slightly surprised me because I heard he was a down-to-earth guy. He was wearing a Navy pea coat, a wool hat, and a scruffy beard.

I introduced myself and told Joel about the angle on our report. I said I would greatly appreciate an interview, that it would really help the piece. He said, "I look so scruffy though." I told him he looked fine and that I was a big fan. Without further hesitation, he agreed. However, the photographer was still getting the marina video. I was worried Joel would want to get out of the cold and cancel the interview. So, I stalled with small talk, telling him I had seen him in concert three times and described my memories of those shows. I was running out of things to say when Todd pulled up.

Joel gave me a terrific interview. I then called the newsroom and spoke to the assignment editor. "The story has started off okay," I under-sold it. "I just interviewed Billy Joel." She didn't believe me until I assured her I wasn't kidding. I heard her yell out to the news staff, "Matt just got Billy Joel." It was pure luck. Just as I heard, Billy Joel was a down-to-earth guy.

When I was a general assignment reporter in New York I was assigned to cover the Rock & Roll Hall of Fame Induction Ceremony a couple of times. One of the celebrities I interviewed there was Dick Clark, the TV legend nicknamed "the World's Oldest Teenager" because of his disposition and youthful appearance. Clark was also a savvy businessman who made millions producing television shows long after he became known for his groundbreaking show, *American Bandstand,* which started in 1957.

Clark was one of the nicest celebrities I met. While my photographer was setting up, he and I talked about the city of Utica, New York, where we both worked early in our careers.

Right before the interview, Clark leaned close to me and whispered, "Please tell your photographer not to shoot me tight. I just flew in from LA and I'm exhausted and it's visible." He looked great to me considering he was sixty. Then I noticed his head was shaking. I understood why he wanted the interview done in a wide shot. I understood better years later when he announced he had Parkinson's disease.

Clark was humble and remembered where he came from, unlike some celebrities I met. They acted like their fame made it okay for them to be rude. Some might have had a bad experience with a reporter, but I never thought that gave them license to be uncooperative to *all* reporters. If you don't want to talk, while that's disappointing to me, it's okay. No need to be a jerk about it—like Art Garfunkel was one night.

It happened at another induction ceremony for the Rock & Roll Hall of Fame. Organizers kept the news media behind a rope outside the Waldorf Astoria Hotel when the VIPs arrived. We were like pigs in a pen. Many famous musicians stopped to answer our questions. The inductees held news conferences inside later, but other attendees gave interviews on the way in. Garfunkel, and what appeared to be a much, much younger woman with him, got out of a limousine and walked towards us. He then stopped on a dime, smiled and said nothing as he turned around and entered the hotel. It wasn't enough to ignore the reporters; he thought it was hilarious that he faked us out. I turned to the other reporters and said, "That's his new version of 'The Sound of Silence.'"

Garfunkel's rudeness notwithstanding, I found most famous musicians, like Joel, were cool with reporters. They appreciated the press.

CHAPTER EIGHT

Gypsies, Trump, and Thieves

SOUND BITE:

"I see evil in your life. I see a curse."

—"Miss Delilah," a fortune-teller, according to three customers
who paid her thousands of dollars

In the early 90s one of my first stories for the Channel 9 I-Team was about fortune-telling gypsies who were taking money from naïve customers. It's one of the oldest scams there is but still around because people continually fall for it. The victims are often depressed or worried about their health or a loved one. Some are lonely hearts who have had bad luck in romantic relationships. Instead of seeing a therapist, they go to alleged fortune-tellers or psychics, hoping their lives will somehow improve. By the time their sessions end, their lives haven't changed, but their bank accounts have.

The scam often works this way: A woman sets up shop in a strip mall or rents a small house or office. She gives herself an exotic name, such as, in this case, "Miss Delilah" (they must think the "Miss" adds respect and credibility). They use various devices, including tarot cards and crystal balls. They tell customers they are the victim of a curse and something terrible is going to happen to them soon. However, the gypsy says she can remove the "curse." For a fee, of course.

The three women who contacted me said Miss Delilah, working out of a small home in Essex County, New Jersey, charged twenty dollars for the first session. She said the curse was so strong that more sessions were needed, and she doubled the price for each one. The "curses" were always "strong," never weak. The women said they lost between $1,000 and $10,000. Then they realized nothing changed in their lives and they had been scammed. They told me they tried to get their money back, but Miss Delilah would not answer the door when she realized the victims were onto her. She would send out a big guy who would tell them she was out of town or sick or give some other excuse.

The women said Miss Delilah instructed them after the first or second session to bring a hardboiled egg to the next reading. She told them she would start to lift the curse through the egg. She'd have them close their eyes while she cracked the egg. When she told them to open their eyes, lo and behold, there would be "blood" spilling out of the egg. Sometimes, it would be a clump of hair or insects.

It's a miracle!

While the customer's eyes were closed the gypsy would replace the egg that the customer brought with one of her own, in which she inserted the fake blood or other props.

After my interviews with the victims, a photographer and I went to the storefront Miss Delilah was using. We wanted to see it from a distance, get the lay of the land and not be seen by her yet because I had a plan: an undercover producer would pose as a customer, wearing a hidden camera. We hoped Miss Delilah would tell the producer that she needed to return with an egg to have the curse lifted. And with more money.

Our undercover shoot worked like a charm. I couldn't have scripted it better, and the video and audio were perfect. The "blood" coming out of the split egg was especially good color.

The next day, my photographer and I were going to knock on the gypsy's door, camera rolling.

We never got that far.

We were about ten feet from the door when a tall, fat, and extremely hairy guy wearing a white tank undershirt came outside. He was screaming, "You stay away from here," and "Get away."

He was also swinging a baseball bat at me. Hard.

He charged us, swinging the bat back and forth nonstop. I couldn't believe he was doing this on camera. People often asked me if I was scared when confronting bad guys. Usually not. Although they might have wanted to punch me out, I always thought they wouldn't do it with a camera rolling. I worried more about mentally unhinged people, like the homeless woman who threw a beer bottle at me.

I was frightened by the bat-swinging maniac, but at the same time I thought about the great video we were getting. It was kind of sick thinking, but I felt pressed to make the story better. I ducked a few times but didn't back away immediately. I wanted him to keep swinging to get more video of it. I then thought I'd better retreat because I realized he wasn't doing this for effect. I wanted the footage but also wanted to keep my head intact.

The bat-swinging video aired several times in the promo for the piece and of course in the report. I included an interview with a detective in the Essex County Sheriff's Office who said fortune-telling was illegal in some states (including New York and New Jersey) when a person receives a fee or compensation for it. But many fortune-tellers avoid the law and angry customers by constantly moving. And they are not the highest priority for many busy law enforcement agencies unless they take large sums of cash.

Miss Delilah was not found or heard from after my report. My guess is she moved and changed her name, maybe more than once. And probably took more money from desperate people.

I interviewed Donald Trump about a half dozen times in the late '80s and '90s. Sometimes one-on-one, sometimes with other reporters. The subject often had nothing to do with his real estate business. It could be about politics or something big that happened in the city. I didn't see the sense in interviewing anyone about the New York political scene who had nothing to do with it. But assignment managers liked getting Trump interviews because he was outspoken, amusing, and spoke in sound bites. He also rarely if ever turned down interview requests. He enjoyed doing them.

He preferred to do interviews in the Trump Tower lobby instead of his office. The lobby was usually crowded with office workers, shoppers, and tourists. I think Trump liked the attention he got there. I noticed that while he talked to me, he often looked around at the crowd. When the interview was in his office, I had to walk through a large adjacent room where numerous secretaries worked. They looked like contestants in the beauty pageant Trump later owned. Almost all of the secretaries were blonde and beautiful. What I remember most from one interview was something on the front of Trump's desk—a sneaker he said was given to him by Shaquille O'Neal, a seven-foot-one, 325-pound star in the National Basketball Association. It was a size twenty-three. Years later when Trump was campaigning for president, he seemed obsessed by size when opponents mocked his small hands. I thought of him showing off O'Neal's sneakers.

Trump was often asked if he wanted to enter politics and always denied it. Despite that, I thought he might run for mayor of New York someday. He talked about politics so often I thought he was laying the groundwork for a run for office. But it never occurred to me he might run for president.

I was at Trump Tower on May 1, 1989, with at least a dozen other reporters for a memorable news conference. The subject was

Trump's comments about the gang rape and assault twelve days earlier of Trisha Meili, a twenty-eight-year-old investment banker who was attacked while jogging in Central Park. It became known nationwide as "the Central Park Jogger" case.

Trump had placed ads in four New York newspapers calling for the state to adopt the death penalty. The ad said in part, "Mayor Koch has stated that hate and rancor should be removed from our hearts. I do not think so. I want to hate these muggers and murderers. They should be forced to suffer."

One of the teenagers, Yusuf Salaam, claimed his family received death threats after the ad was published.

Trump said the same things about the suspects at the news conference as he wrote in his ad.

The "Central Park Five" were convicted and sentenced to prison; their sentences ranged from five to fifteen years. They said the police coerced them into confessing.

There was a problem with the convictions and Trump's comments: the accused didn't do it. Their convictions were vacated in 2002 after a convicted murderer and serial rapist named Matias Reyes confessed to the crime and said he acted alone. DNA evidence confirmed Reyes was the sole participant. By then, the Central Park Five had spent years in prison. They city paid them $41 million to settle their civil rights lawsuits.

Salaam called Trump "the fire starter" in a 2016 story in *The Guardian*. When a film about the case was released on Netflix in 2019, Manhattan district attorney Cyrus Vance Jr. said the men "were wrongfully convicted and what happened to them was an injustice."

By then, of course, Donald Trump was president. He declined to apologize about the harsh comments he made concerning the five black and Latino men who were wrongly convicted. He said, "You have people on both sides of that." I think he meant some people still believed the Central Park Five were guilty, despite the DNA evidence linking Reyes and his confession that he acted alone.

It was reminiscent of what Trump said in 2017 after a white supremacist drove his car into a crowd at a "Unite the White" rally in Charlottesville, Virginia, and killed a woman. Trump famously said, "You also had people that were very fine people on both sides."

Regardless of how you feel about Trump, I have never seen or heard him say "I'm wrong" or "I apologize," about anything.

I opened a report in August 2016 when working at KVOA-TV in Tucson with this sound bite: "If I win, I will remember the people of Tucson. I will remember the people of Arizona." It was Trump speaking at a rally earlier that year in the Tucson Convention Center.

I said in my voice-over, "Donald Trump told supporters he will remember Tucson, but his campaign has not paid Tucson."

I received a tip from a Tucson city official that the Trump for President campaign owed the city nearly $82,000. The bill was for the police department providing security for Trump's rally.

My source said Democratic presidential candidate Bernie Sanders also hadn't paid for police protection at his rally a day earlier at the convention center. The senator's campaign owed the city $44,000.

I sent a public records request to the city, and the documents confirmed what my source told me. The campaigns of the two wealthy men owed the city a total of $126,000. That's not a lot in the scheme of things for most larger cities, but it was significant in Tucson, one of the country's poorest. As one councilman told me, "We have a severe shortage of police officers, and $126,000 could be used to hire three cops."

I first reported this in a story we called "Unpaid & Overdue." Even before it aired, I heard from many angry viewers. They saw the fifteen-second promo and thought the story would be one-sided. Of course, I reported on both Trump's and Sanders's debts. Judging reports before they aired happened often, especially from people who saw the promo on Facebook or Twitter. Then when the story aired they realized I reported the unpaid bills on both sides.

From 2016 until 2020, I heard from more angry viewers than in the previous forty years combined. Especially about political pieces. Republicans and Democrats used to be civil to each other despite their differences. Over the past four years it's been like a civil war between them.

People from both parties agreed about this story. They felt the city had been used and I concurred. The candidates came in to try to get votes, used city resources, and failed to pay up. The city attorney Mike Rankin sent letters to the campaigns demanding payment.

Sanders's campaign responded to Rankin with a letter of its own, saying, "The Campaign did not contract for, nor did it request or arrange for the Tucson Police Department to provide public safety at the Campaign event." Sanders's attorney said the city "should discuss cost-sharing matters directly with the Secret Service."

Trump's campaign sent a similar letter.

Tucson councilman Steve Kozachik told me that in the future the city should demand payment up front. "Any political candidate coming into any jurisdiction is responsible for paying the full cost of them showing up," Kozachik said. "Otherwise it's a political gift. And governments can't give political gifts away."

Both campaigns still hadn't paid the city a dime three months later. I wanted to keep the pressure on city officials to do something to help taxpayers. Council needed to change the billing policy regarding campaign events. I thought Tucson's lawmakers were being taken for country bumpkins by the candidates' high-powered, big-city lawyers. I think investigative reporters need to do follow-ups even when nothing has changed in a story like this one. Reporters need to keep the pressure on elected officials—remind the public that these officials brought up changing a policy when the story was hot, but then did nothing.

After I did three stories about this, discussions began among the mayor and council about requiring an up-front payment. Several months later, a new policy was adopted: anticipated costs for security, traffic, and public safety would be identified by city officials and put in agreements to use a city facility. Those costs would be part of a required deposit. If the campaign refused to pay the deposit, there would be no rally. I thought it could lead to an interesting showdown between the city and President Trump or another candidate.

The two millionaires never paid their bills for their 2016 rallies, but a significant change had occurred. I was gratified and so were taxpayers I spoke with. If I hadn't held city officials accountable, maybe the policy change would not have been made. The story might have been forgotten.

Tucson Mayor Jonathan Rothschild told me in 2016 that he heard from other mayors that Trump didn't pay their cities. In the summer of 2019, the Center for Public Integrity did an investigation to see if anything had changed. It reported that Trump's campaign still "owed 10 city governments from Arizona to Pennsylvania at least $841,219." I called the ten cities, confirmed it and did a piece on it. Trump's campaign attorney again said the expenses for security weren't the campaign's responsibility.

Ruth Cording was thrilled when a man named Greg Bryant visited her Tucson home and said he could help her get almost $1,200 a month from a Veterans Administration benefit. Ruth was a retired eight-four-year-old widow living on a fixed income. Bryant told Ruth the benefit was part of a "secret government program."

It was secret alright. So secret even the government didn't know about it.

Ruth had been living alone for three years when we met in 2017. Her husband, David, served in the Air Force for twenty years. They met when they were twelve years old and went to Tucson High School together. They were married for sixty-four years.

"He was a fantastic man," Ruth told me. "He was the best husband a wife could have."

It was against this backdrop that Ruth's son, Dan, called me, suspicious about his mom's recent visitor. Dan wasn't at Ruth's home when Bryant first showed up, but Ruth showed him documents Bryant had given her for what was labeled a "VA Pension Benefit." At the end of the presentation, Bryant told Ruth there was going to be an application fee of $1,495. "That's when alarm bells went off in my head," Dan said.

Fortunately, Ruth didn't sign any of the papers that Bryant put in front of her. She was interested, however. She told Bryant to return the next day when her son could be there.

"I have a weakness to trust people. And goodness sakes, twelve hundred dollars a month would just be a dream," she told me on camera.

After I received the call from Ruth's brother, I contacted VA officials and researched the issue. I learned that only accredited agents and attorneys could charge fees for assisting in an appeal of a case, not for a basic claim. The officials told me they had no record of Greg Bryant being accredited.

I told Ruth and Dan Cording this, then asked if we could be at Ruth's house when Bryant returned. They said sure. The next day, the photographer and I were hiding in an adjacent room, listening and recording while Bryant delivered his sales pitch. About twenty minutes later, after hearing Bryant mention the application fee a few times, we approached him, camera rolling. He remained seated and seemed calm.

Bryant said he had "helped one hundred people" get VA benefits over the past five years through his company.

I told him, "If you charge a fee, you have to be accredited, and the VA did not find you in the system." He said, "No, I don't. I don't have to be accredited." When I again told him he had to be accredited he replied, "I'm a private company and I have clients." He said he makes his money from the $1,495 application fee.

I replied, "You're not ripping off elderly people and widows, are you?"

"Nope," he said. "Because if I was, I'd be in jail by now." *The way many prosecutors handle low-profile white-collar crimes,* I thought, *not necessarily.*

I asked Bryant, "Do you have your list of references here, or can you send me some?" He answered, "Why would I send you a list of my references? Are you going to sign up for the program?" A sarcastic answer, and good TV. He was clearly getting agitated.

I said, "You just mentioned you have at least one hundred happy customers, so I was just asking if you could show that to me."

He replied, "I didn't necessarily say they were happy." Another good line. At least the guy had a sense of humor. I had to try hard to hold back a laugh. He added, "But why would I give you a list of my references?" I was thinking, *Because any reputable businesses would provide references.*

Here's the rest of our exchange:

Me: "Do you own the company?"

Bryant: "I don't need to answer that question."

Me "Why not? A legitimate businessperson would say who owns the company that he or she is working for."

Bryant: "I don't need to answer that question."

Me: "To whom do you answer to, sir? If you don't own the company, who is your superior, your boss?"

Bryant: "I answer to God."

He hit the trifecta. Three entertaining answers! While saying that, Bryant stood up and said, "I'm not answering any more of your questions." He then walked out of Ruth's home.

Dan Cording said, "There are widows of veterans that are struggling. I mean, it's unconscionable. I just can't imagine doing that to somebody."

Ruth told me, "I am angry, and I'm not a cursing person, but I'm mad as hell."

I interviewed Drew Early, an attorney who specialized in elder law. He said there were many unaccredited and thus unsupervised agents around the country—salesmen who never took the accreditation test and make mistakes that could be costly to people like Ruth Cording. Early said, "The greatest danger I think is she could incur an overpayment, a debt, back to the US government. And the US government will seek debt recovery."

I ended the report by saying that the VA and veterans service organizations offer free help in applying for the benefit that Greg Bryant was selling. It's called the "Aid and Attendance Benefit."

A couple of friends asked me if I felt sneaky about hiding in a back room while listening to Bryant's sales pitch. Not at all. Although I had no reason to disbelieve what Ruth and her son claimed, I needed to hear it directly from Bryant. I doubted that if I called him to request an interview, he would say, "Yeah, I am not accredited and charge for a service people can get without any charge." I had to get proof, and there was no other way to get it. Hidden microphones and undercover cameras are invaluable tools for reporters, especially when there are no documents or other evidence. Think of how many news stories you've seen that without the video or audio proof, there would be no case against scammers and criminals.

In the end, the public was warned. There's no need or reason to pay $1,495 for something that's available for free. I never heard from Greg Bryant again.

CHAPTER NINE

Medical Mistakes

S O U N D   B I T E :

"She used to dance a lot; she was the life of the party. Now, she's in a wheelchair and has one leg."

—Stella Johnson, talking about her mother, Luz Huertas

People Are Fascinated By Stories about medical mistakes. I think it was because viewers don't like the holier-than-thou dispositions some doctors have. Those stories are difficult to get approved by management because stations are afraid of getting sued by doctors with deep pockets. But sometimes when you have all the proof that a mistake was indeed made, the station's management and lawyer will give you the green light. Two such reports seemed to be popular with viewers, judging by the number of calls the station and I received afterwards.

I got the go-ahead to do a piece on a terrible mistake involving a woman named Luz Huertas of Bergen County, New Jersey. Luz didn't speak English and I don't speak Spanish (which would have helped working in New York, Tampa and Tucson).

Luz had agonizing pain in her right knee. Her daughter, Stella Johnson, told me Luz had three surgeries at Holy Name Hospital in Teaneck, New Jersey, that did not alleviate the pain. We had records showing that during the third surgery, her orthopedist lacerated an artery in her right leg. The damage was so severe the leg had to be amputated.

I found Luz's doctor in his car outside his office and approached him. I asked, "Would you please tell me what happened to Luz Huertas?" He shook his head, said no, and drove off. His lawyer and the hospital also declined comment.

I learned that the medical society's website named only doctors who made three or more significant mistakes. I said on the air, "Doctors could commit two horrible errors and you'd never know it." Critics said the medical society cared more about protecting its members than protecting the public. I agree.

When I interviewed the VP of the medical society, he said, "The point of the matter is it is hard to put on every single profile of every single doctor every single issue that may have reached the point of settlement."

I wasn't buying it. I asked why. He said, "Because that then adds to that mass of information the patient has to go through."

It was a weak answer, and our viewers knew it, judging by the comments I received. People looking for a good doctor are willing to search through a "mass of information." It's a lot easier than losing a leg.

Luz Huertas filed a malpractice suit against her orthopedic surgeon and the hospital. It was settled out of court, which happens in roughly 90 percent of these cases. The amount of money she received was not disclosed. How much is a leg worth?

Another medical mistake I reported involved a man whose wife called me after he nearly died.

The eighty-one-year-old Long Island resident (who wanted to remain anonymous, so we blurred his face) had open-heart surgery. More than two months later he was having severe stomach pain and digestive problems. Doctors said they couldn't figure out why. Then, after the man was taken to the emergency room with excruciating stomach pain, one doctor had the sense to take X-rays.

A surgical towel was found inside the patient. It had been there since his open-heart surgery eighty-three days earlier. Immediate surgery to remove it was ordered.

This is not as uncommon as you might think. Research shows that surgical instruments are left inside as many as 6,000 patients each year in the US. Besides towels, they include scalpels, scissors, needles, and clamps.

Hospitals have taken steps to alleviate the problem, including the use of radio-frequency tags. But it still happens, often due to carelessness and the assembly line of surgeries in so many hospitals.

The Long Island man survived and sued the hospital. An undisclosed, out-of-court settlement was reached.

CHAPTER TEN

Towing Trouble

SOUND BITE:

"It's been very devastating because I had to buy another car."

—Gloria McNair, whose car's transmission was ruined by a towing company

Unscrupulous towing companies operated everywhere I worked. They towed cars for no legitimate reason. They charged exorbitant storage fees. And they occasionally damaged cars they towed.

The car owned by Long Island couple Gloria and Wayne McNair was towed after it broke down. The towing company used a regular truck instead of a flatbed to transport the car. That ruined the transmission. The repair estimate was $3,600.

The owner of the towing company, Safeway Towing, refused to pay to fix the transmission. The McNairs took the company and its owner to court and won. With court costs they were due $4,160.44.

At least, they thought they had won.

"We got a big runaround," Wayne told me. "Red tape."

Two years went by and the McNairs still weren't paid. During that time their teenaged son died of a rare disease and Wayne lost his job.

Then they called me. I found out by checking New York State records that "Safeway Towing" was not the business's legal name. It was "Elite Towing." As we showed in the piece, "Safeway Towing" was on their trucks, the signs at their garage and in the Yellow Pages (remember them?). So, the McNairs sued "Safeway Towing." They couldn't afford an attorney and didn't think of checking county or state business records.

When the owner hadn't paid the couple promptly, sheriff's deputies tried to serve him but couldn't enforce the court order because it contained the company's incorrect legal name. Seemed to me like a sneaky way of doing business. Even the sheriff's department's spokesperson told me, "These people were victimized a second time." I told the McNairs the company's legal name was "Elite Towing." Wayne said, "I didn't know anything [about the legal name] until after we got the papers back from the sheriff's department saying, 'All assets belong to 'Elite Towing.'"

They took Elite to court and won again. But two months after the verdict, the towing company owner still hadn't paid up. So, I paid him a visit.

When I approached the owner at the garage, he walked away. My photographer and I followed him as he walked from the garage to his office. I asked, "Why are you walking away?" He mumbled something about it being his insurance company's fault. Typical pass-the-buck stuff I heard frequently from business owners who were delinquent on payments to customers. It was never their fault.

A few days after I confronted the towing company owner, the McNairs called me. They received a check that day for $4,160.44, the entire amount they were owed.

I went to their home for the happy ending. They showed me the check and Gloria said, "We are so, so happy. You really made this happen for us." Wayne interjected, "You should give him a hug." Gloria hugged me, then Wayne said, "I want a hug, too," and we embraced.

After we showed the hugs, I ended the piece with this line: "The McNairs then drove off, not into the sunset, but to the bank."

I was pleased I helped them and included information that not all consumers knew: when suing a business, find out its legal name.

PART II

Tampa Confessions

2005–2009

CHAPTER ELEVEN

Doctors, Painkillers, and Deaths

SOUND BITE:

"I give Dr. Hays a hundred dollars and a hug and he gives me whatever I want."

—A young Tampa woman addicted to painkillers

While working at WFTS in Tampa in 2008, I learned about "pill mills" and their often-tragic consequences. By then it had been well documented that Florida was the opioid capital of the US. People addicted to prescription painkillers drove from far away to buy pills and darken their lives in the Sunshine State.

Florida had become the destination of choice for addicts and drug dealers because there was little regulation of its pain-management clinics. Other states had established computerized systems that tracked the sale of legal narcotics, but Florida did not. Many investigators and victims' loved ones appealed to state lawmakers. But nothing happened for years. The strong suspicion was that many lawmakers were in bed with the pharmaceutical companies, who had become major players in Florida politics.

71

The addicts knew that doctors at many walk-in clinics took cash payments and asked no questions before providing massive doses of painkillers. No medical records or examinations were requested. Their philosophy was, "You have the cash? We have the pills." The pill mills in Florida started in the 1990s and began proliferating in about 2003. It was all done in the open with little oversight. That last part angered me. What the hell were lawmakers doing?

I wanted to do a story that put faces on the victims and doctors. I had seen several investigative reports about the problem, but not one in the Tampa market that caught a doctor red-handed or prompted politicians to act.

I received several complaints about a pain-management doctor named Richard Hays. He worked at the Kenaday Medical Clinic. It had a convenient location on Tampa's busiest street, and was a very busy office. The first complaint came from a woman pleading for help. Her twenty-one-year-old daughter was addicted to painkillers, and her mother was afraid she would die from an overdose. The mom told me she knew other former patients of Hays and their families who would attest to his overprescribing.

I contacted two law enforcement sources who said off the record that they knew about Hays. They said he recklessly and routinely overprescribed painkillers. They were frustrated that they weren't given the go-ahead from those with prosecutorial powers to raid Hays's office and seize his records.

Of course, I couldn't just take the word of those alleged complaints about Hays. I needed proof. So, my producer and I spent hours in the medical examiner's office reviewing every autopsy and police report in Hillsborough County (where Hays's office was) and adjacent Pinellas County. The records showed Hays had written prescriptions for six people who died of overdoses in 2007, more than any other doctor in those counties.

The young woman whose mother called me agreed to an interview with her face blurred. She was afraid that one of Hays's current patients might hurt her if they saw her complaining on TV. She said, "He's very, very popular among that addicted community."

We called her "Sue." She was very pretty, with blonde hair and blue eyes. She was a part-time college student and worked as a waitress. But she had trouble showing up for classes and work because she spent most of her days sleeping.

Sue said she was getting pills from Dr. Hays for more than two years. She claimed he often changed offices. We learned that Hays worked as an "independent contractor" in at least three pain-management clinics.

Sue said she started taking painkillers after she hurt her back in a car accident in high school five years earlier, and the addiction soon followed. That's how it starts for many people. Sue said during her first visit with Hays, he barely looked at her records and MRI. He told her he took cash only, $300 up front, $100 every visit thereafter. Those were just his appointment fees; the pills were extra.

"I did put the pills in my mouth," Sue said. "And I kept coming back. But he never once told me no."

Sue was trying to stop taking pills and wanted the public to know about Hays. She gave me her customer history report. It listed all the prescriptions Hays wrote for her from one pharmacy over a two-year period. One period on the report stood out.

On August 8, 2006, Hays prescribed her 150 oxycodone tablets, at thirty milligrams each. Two weeks later, he prescribed 360 oxycodone. On September 9, another 300 oxycodone. So, in a thirty-one-day period, Hays prescribed Sue 810 oxycodone pills. She could take twenty-six pills a day and still have a few left over.

I showed her customer history report on camera to three experts (with her name redacted to protect her privacy). Bill Janes, director of the Florida Office of Drug Control, said, "It's unethical, and that person should not be allowed to practice." A longtime pharmacist named Bob Parrado told me, "That has a 'wow' factor." I asked, "In what way specifically?" He said, "It very easily could have killed this young woman."

Dr. Rafael Miguel, director of the University of South Florida Pain Management Program, said 240 oxycodone, at thirty milligrams each, would be a lot in one month. Remember, Hays prescribed Sue 810 tablets. "What you just showed me here," Dr. Miguel said, "you show this to ten other bona fide, board-certified pain doctors, they would tell you, 'That's a drug dealer.' In no other terms. You can't mince words here."

I thought, *Thank you for your candor, Dr. Miguel. Not many doctors publicly criticize another doctor*—much like cops and the "blue wall of silence" some of them adhere to.

Another complaint about Hays came from Alice Engel. Her thirty-eight-year-old daughter, Denise, died of an accidental drug overdose in their Tampa home in 2007. The police report said a bottle containing 141 Percocet tablets (the brand name for oxycodone) was found in Denise's bedroom. The death certificate said Denise died due to the combined effects of four drugs. Percocet was one of them.

It had been prescribed four days earlier by Dr. Richard Hays.

Denise's mother said, "He gave her four or five prescriptions at one time. I think he should be put out of practice and put in jail."

After I did the interviews and had the records, my photographer and I went to Hays's home. We sat in our unmarked SUV for several hours and there was no sign of him. I didn't want to knock on his door because I was virtually certain he'd slam it in my face, especially when I showed him the records I had. How could he defend prescribing 810 oxycodone in a month to one patient?

We went to the Kenaday Medical clinic early the next morning and waited. He arrived at around 8:30. He wore a white medical jacket and a rumpled look. He was short and overweight. His shirt was falling out of his pants, his red hair disheveled. He appeared calm, even stoic, considering a reporter and photographer greeted him outside his office.

I introduced myself and said, "I wanted to ask you some questions about your practice."

Speaking low and very, very slowly, he said, "I can't right now."

I said, "Why not?"

He replied, "I'm busy." He dragged out those two words. It sounded to me like his speech was slurred.

I kept walking alongside him and asked, "Will you look at this customer history report?" I knew he'd probably continue walking into the clinic but hoped that question might stir his curiosity; maybe he'd wonder whose report I had. But he said nothing more and walked inside.

I later called Hays's attorney. He refused to allow Hays to do an interview and declined one himself.

I was disappointed but not surprised. How could Hays or his lawyer defend the massive overprescribing? I hounded investigators about why this guy was still practicing and kept hearing, "We know about Hays and we are working on a case against him." I often got angry about businesses staying open while everyone, including the authorities, knew they were ripping off people. I was impatient with the slowness of the system. I thought Hays was a doctor who cared more about money than his patients' well-being. I thought it was a travesty that he was allowed to continue to practice. Yes, the patients took the pills, but in my opinion Hays was an enabler. I thought it was like selling guns with no background checks. In these cases pills were the weapon.

I mentioned in the piece the growing support among lawmakers to establish a prescription drug–monitoring system that was instituted in other states. A database in those states was aimed at tracking sales of prescription drugs containing controlled substances, such as painkillers. The idea was to help law enforcement, pharmacists, and doctors detect patients who were getting drugs from multiple sources at once or a few days apart.

By 2009, authorities counted more than 900 pill mills in Florida. A prescription drug–monitoring system was established. Lawmakers in the Sunshine State finally saw the light.

In November 2011, almost exactly three years after my investigation of Hays, drug agents raided a medical office in Kissimmee, Florida, near Orlando. Investigators with the Florida Department of Law Enforcement had collected evidence and talked to patients about a doctor there overprescribing painkillers. The physician was suspected of prescribing more than 800,000 oxycodone tablets to patients over the past two years.

The doctor was Richard Hays.

Department of Health records showed Hays was repeatedly accused of improperly prescribing painkillers. The agency had filed three administrative complaints against him. In April 2012, Hays voluntarily relinquished his medical license and avoided a possible prison sentence. He was never criminally charged. In 2019, no one in Florida's attorney general office, the Osceola county attorney's office, or the Florida Department of Law Enforcement would tell me why Hays was never prosecuted.

Hays's license relinquishment came three years too late for the woman we interviewed, the woman we called "Sue." In 2009, a year after my report, her mother called me.

Sue had died from an accidental drug overdose. She was twenty-two years old.

I thought if a lawmaker's child had died from an overdose, God forbid, a drug-monitoring system might have been established sooner. Maybe it would have saved Sue's life. I couldn't stop thinking about her and her parents for a long time. While preparing to write this book, I watched the report for the first time in ten years. I was haunted by seeing her. I'm glad her face was blurred; seeing it would haunt me even more.

CHAPTER TWELVE

Loafing Deputies

SOUND BITE:

"It's certainly not an effective use of personnel."

—A Hillsborough County (Florida) chief deputy sheriff, about deputies we caught loafing

Stories I reported about people caught sleeping or otherwise loafing on the job were popular with viewers. When the loafers were government employees, taxpayers were especially angry. Viewers would say, "I'm not paying taxes for that guy to loaf on the job." An investigation I did in Tampa in 2008 about loafing deputies created tremendous viewer interest, and a lot of headaches for me.

Three people had called me independently, each saying they saw deputies from the Hillsborough County Sheriff's Office sitting in their patrol cars in a church parking lot for hours at a time. They claimed that when it wasn't too hot the deputies would stand outside and chat. One caller said he saw them playing Frisbee. In uniform, on taxpayers' time.

Photographer Randy Wright and I went to the location in Wimauma, thirty miles southeast of Tampa, for seven days without taking out the camera. We only had about fifteen minutes a day in between other stories. Every day we saw between two and four deputies' patrol cars parked behind the church. We thought the story was worth checking out further with a camera.

I discussed this with my news director, who agreed we would have to observe the deputies over an extended period. One problem with investigative reporting at many stations is management doesn't give reporters enough time to do the "big" investigations, those that can't be done properly in a couple of days. Like most investigative reporters, I had to juggle the long-term investigations with the less complicated, quick-hit assignments. But I had the go-ahead, and a plan.

The church parking lot where the deputies' cars were parked could be clearly seen from an adjacent golf course. There were tall trees between the lot and the course, but there were enough openings between the trees to give Randy a clear shot. I asked the golf course owner if we could stand on his property to get video "for a story." He asked, "What's the story about?" I told him about the tips we received and how it wouldn't be fair to the deputies if we reported it without extended observation. I knew I was taking a chance by giving the property owner the details. Maybe he wouldn't want to be involved or would be afraid of backlash from the sheriff's department. Maybe he'd tip off the deputies and they'd leave, killing our story. But he gave us his approval.

Randy started shooting on a steamy, late summer day. Besides my reporter's notebook, I brought a lawn chair and a stopwatch. When we arrived, we saw four patrol cars parked behind the church, out of view of passing cars. Randy looked through the camera's viewfinder, zoomed in, and gave me the number of each car. There were always at least two cars there between 2 p.m. and 7 p.m., and usually three or four vehicles. We spent five days observing and recording, at least four hours each day. I wrote down the number of every patrol car and kept a record of exactly how long each was there. One car, occupied by a corporal, was parked for nineteen hours and twenty-nine minutes, an average of almost four hours a day. That was one-third of his daily shift.

After five days we had all the footage we needed. I then approached the corporal's car with the camera rolling. Here was our exchange:

> **Corporal:** "Sir, can we help you?"
>
> **Me:** "Is something going on here? Is this a staging area or something?"
>
> **Corporal:** "We're reading reports. What'd you need here, bud?" (Sounding annoyed.)
>
> **Me:** "We got some questions and complaints from viewers who say they see a lot of cars here every day. And I just wondered, is anything going on?"
>
> **Corporal:** "Ah, I know what this is about. Okay." (I had no idea what he meant by that.)
>
> **Me:** "What?"
>
> **Corporal:** "Gotta go."
>
> **Me:** "We actually taped you here for five days for four hours a day or so at a time"
>
> **Corporal:** "That's fine, that's fine, that's fine."
>
> **Me:** "Can you just tell us what you're doing here? Is there a problem? Is there a reason you can tell the taxpayers why you're here four hours at a time?"

The corporal drove away.

I returned to the station, told my news director about the exchange, screened the video and wrote the script. The piece was scheduled to air several days later, on Sunday, October 1, 2006, at 11 p.m. The sunday night 11 o'clock show was among the station's highest rated newscasts most weeks.

My pride over the story soon turned to dismay when it was delayed because we had not interviewed Hillsborough County sheriff

David Gee, despite attempts to do so.

Weeks earlier, I had requested an interview with the sheriff. I wanted to show him our footage and the records of the hours the patrol cars sat in the parking lot. We were told he was "unavailable." Law enforcement often used that word, instead of "declined" or "no comment." Saying "unavailable" might have some viewers thinking the officer would talk if he or she had time. And it sounds a lot better than the truth, which was often that they "refused" to talk.

The promo for the piece began running two days before it was initially scheduled to air. Within hours, someone from the sheriff's department called my boss. The spokesman said a sheriff's representative now wanted to be interviewed for the story. My news director then called me. The piece was being pushed back. I thought it was wrong. We had given the department more than two weeks' notice of what we had.

The news director was a nice enough guy but didn't strike me as the type to stand up to those he perceived as powerful. I thought he should have stuck up for me and told the sheriff's people, "Matthew asked you for an interview two weeks ago. It's too late now." And I would have said that on the air.

The sheriff's department trotted out its number two man, Chief Deputy Jose Docobo, to do the interview. The story ran a week after its scheduled air date. Turned out, it was a stronger piece with the department interview, because Docobo surprised me. He said, "Three and a half, four hours does seem to be an excessive amount of time for any one deputy to be in a location. We will certainly specifically address the individuals you've identified and find out exactly what was going on. And if they were not acting appropriately, we'll take whatever action we need to take to correct it."

I thought it was an honest answer. If I were doing public relations, that's exactly what I'd recommend he say.

I later heard that the department separated the schmoozing deputies by transferring them to other districts.

CHAPTER THIRTEEN

Lying on Camera

SOUND BITE:

"I never said that. I know I didn't say that."

—Linda Bollea, then the wife of professional wrestler Hulk Hogan,
denying things she said

Every good investigative reporter I know has caught someone lying on camera. Some experienced reporters have caught many people lying. We caught someone in 2007 and it couldn't have been more obvious. It was uncomfortable for me. It was also great TV.

The story involved the family of wrestler Hulk Hogan (real name Terry Jean Bollea). Hogan's seventeen-year-old son, Nick, had been in a car crash in Clearwater that left a friend in a coma. Police said Nick Hogan was speeding when his Toyota Supra smashed into a palm tree. He was charged with felony reckless driving.

The Hogans gave me their first interview since the crash. I got it because I worked with their attorney on other stories and we had a good relationship. A few days before the interview, out of nowhere, a guy called me who said he had a video I'd want to see. He said it showed Hulk's wife, Linda, and daughter, Brooke, drag racing on Florida streets. The scene was part of a 2005 documentary titled *Vehicular Lunatics.* The anonymous caller gave me the director's name. I found him and he gave me a copy. All he wanted was the documentary's title mentioned in the report. I said I'd be happy to mention it if I decided to use it.

In the video, Nick Hogan's mom and sister are in a car at night, stopped at a light alongside another car. Brooke is behind the wheel. She yells to the other, unseen driver, "You ready? Let's do this!" She then speeds off. Later, Linda Bollea is asked on camera how she feels about street racing. She says, "Oh, I love it, I love it. The rush. The speed on the roads. Stereo blasting. Heart pounding. Racing between other cars. Dodging the cops. It's awesome." Her son, Nick, is standing nearby, smiling.

I was stunned. And after covering 9/11 and working so long in New York, almost nothing stunned me.

Before the crash that critically injured his friend, Nick Hogan had been arrested four times for speeding. We had video from a police car dashboard camera of one of those arrests. I felt it was important to let viewers decide if the apple did not fall far from the tree, as I certainly felt. Here was a teenager with a history of driving too fast, about to go to court for getting into a violent wreck while street racing. A young man whose mother was filmed street racing and saying how much she loved it. She said so with her son listening.

Near the end of my interview with the Hogans, with their two attorneys watching from off camera (including my source), I tell the family I've seen this scene in *Vehicular Lunatics.* I read Linda her comments. Before she can answer Nick interjects, "She didn't say that." Then Linda says, "I never said that, 'cause I would never have said that and I know I didn't say that." I tell them it's on tape and unless it was somehow edited, it's clear. There were no cutaways in that interview in *Vehicular Lunatics* in which her comments could have been edited. She was on camera when making those statements.

Immediately after Linda denied in our interview that she made the comments in the documentary, I went right back to the documentary. In the business, that's called "butting" the bite. You see her telling me "I never said that, I know I didn't say that," and it cuts straight to her documentary quotes. It was powerful stuff.

The interview ended on that note. There was an awkward silence in the room while my crew packed up the gear. I felt uncomfortable, but knew I had asked the right questions.

The lawyer who facilitated the interview was very upset with me. Hulk Hogan, all six feet, seven inches and 300 pounds of him, was also not pleased. He just shook his head and mumbled something I couldn't make out. The lawyer said if he knew I had seen the documentary and was going to ask those questions, he wouldn't have approved the interview. I told him that's exactly why I didn't tell him in advance. I felt a little guilty, almost sneaky, but only for a few seconds. I reminded myself about my obligation to report the story I felt viewers needed to see. Journalists are under no obligation to tell interviewees or their associates everything they are going to ask.

The report was picked up by TMZ** and dozens of other outlets. A popular Tampa radio station played the entire piece the next morning. The cohosts were incredulous about Linda's denying to me the comments she made in the documentary.

I didn't report what happened after the interview.

While I was waiting outside the Hogans' home for my crew to pack up the van for the ride back to the station, Hulk approached me. It was pitch black out, and with no camera rolling I was afraid of what he might do.

He began crying.

He was emotional not only because of the interview. He said his wife was about to divorce him and now his son was in trouble because of the crash and his world was falling apart. I couldn't believe

* https://www.tmz.com/2007/11/20/hogan-family-vehicular-lunatics/

this world-famous giant of a man was almost crying on my shoulder. I was surprised he would share this with me, a relative stranger. We had met once years earlier when I interviewed him and Mr. T near Madison Square Garden for a funny wrestling piece. I tried to lighten the mood by reminding him of that, but the guy's done a million interviews and didn't remember it. He said he wished I didn't ask Linda about *Vehicular Lunatics.* I think he thought it could hurt Nick's upcoming case, but he didn't threaten or try to intimidate me. I told him I had to ask Linda about her contradictory comments considering their son's driving record.

Nick Hogan accepted a plea deal for reckless driving and was sentenced to only eight months in jail. A less famous person without a wealthy father might have received more time.

Nick Hogan's friend, who suffered severe brain damage, was still living as of late 2019.

My source, the lawyer who arranged the interview, never spoke to me again. I could live with that. I could not look myself in the mirror if I failed to ask Linda about her comments.

PART III

Tucson Confessions

2013-2020

CHAPTER FOURTEEN

Going to the Dogs

SOUND BITE:

"I'm not answering any more questions. And you know what else? Fuck you!"

—A trainer at Tucson Greyhound Park when I asked him about drugging a dog

TV stations have lots of turnover in management. And with that often comes turnover in personnel. After it happened to me in New York, it happened again in Tampa.

For four years I had been "on the beach," an industry term meaning out of work in TV. I filled in that time working a barnesandnoble. com gig and two years in public relations. The silver lining was I had plenty of time with my two sons and daughter. The boys played baseball, and each received college scholarships; one was drafted by the Chicago White Sox in 2010 and spent several years in the minors. And my daughter received an academic college scholarship.

Family life was good, but professionally I was bored out of my mind. Then Tucson called. My agent said the NBC affiliate KVOA wanted an investigative reporter who would "shake the tree" to arouse people to action or reaction.

89

When I started work in the "Old Pueblo," I was fifty-nine, about twice as old as the reporters at the station. I was self-conscious about my graying hair, just as I was in New York about going bald. So, instead of masking my thinning strands under another tawdry toupee, I dyed them. Like detecting toupees, I usually could tell when guys dyed their hair. It was too dark and looked phony. I eventually thought mine was both, and after a couple of years I let the gray back in. My better half, Susan, said I looked "distinguished." Ha. I've never looked back.

My first story in Tucson was about dogs being mistreated. I love dogs, and my family almost always had one when I was growing up. Now I get dogs only from shelters and rescues. I think people who buy from a breeder or pet store are either self-centered or ignorant, sometimes both. Years ago, I was ignorant about this and bought a dog from a breeder. Why would anyone buy from one of those places while there are thousands of homeless dogs at shelters?

I always liked doing stories that speak for these wonderful creatures who can't speak for themselves. I've done several reports on irresponsible dog owners who let their pets run in the streets without a leash. The dogs often get hit by a car and killed or seriously injured. All because of someone who never should have been a dog owner. I've done stories about abandoned dogs. Their owners were too lazy to take proper care of them, or couldn't afford a veterinarian's bill. Instead of dropping their dog off at a shelter, they simply abandoned them. I wanted to scream on TV, "PEOPLE, HAVING A PET COSTS MONEY. DON'T GET ONE JUST BECAUSE YOU THINK HE OR SHE IS CUTE. DON'T GET ONE IF YOU CAN'T AFFORD ONE."

Just days after starting work in Tucson in April 2013, I received a tip from a dog lover. She despised greyhound racing in general and Tucson Greyhound Park in particular. She claimed she had information that dogs at the track were being abused. I was very interested in learning more.

This was just the type of story I was hired for. Within days of my arrival, I think I gave the "tree" a good, hard shake.

The tipster gave me records she obtained through a public records request with the Arizona Department of Gaming. They showed that a trainer named Willie Eyler had given a greyhound an anabolic steroid before a race to get him to run faster; that's illegal. The dog won that race.

I requested the track's records from the state because I wanted to obtain them directly and make sure what the tipster gave me were entire, unedited records. The documents I received were identical.

We couldn't find a phone number for Eyler, but we found his address. When we went there, we saw him get in his car outside his mobile home. We approached him with camera rolling. He answered some softball questions before I asked about him drugging the dog. He calmly denied it. He grew angry when I showed him I had the official state records, which included lab results. After I asked several times how the results could be wrong, he said, "I'm done answering your questions." Before he rolled up his window, he said, "And you know what else? Fuck you!"

He then gave me the finger and sped off. Great TV. I couldn't be happier.

Photographer Paul Hanke turned to me and said, "Was I supposed to be rolling on that?" It was a funny line—sarcastic, of course—and the video looked great. I always appreciated a photographer's sense of humor, especially since we spent so much time together. Hanke and I were like an old married couple. We could finish each other's sentences and argued occasionally about our stories, something passionate journalists do because they care.

The greyhound trainer was fined $1,000 by the state and suspended for sixty days. Later, I got another tip about Eyler. Turned out he refused to submit to drug tests. I did a second report on him with new records from the state. Not long after that piece, Eyler was banned from racing in Arizona for life. As often happens, this story prompted tips from viewers who had inside information. We did a third public records request and found that several dogs that raced at TGP were either missing or injured, and that one was dead.

Our reports drew the attention of GREY2K USA, the largest greyhound protection organization in the world. The group joined local activists from Tucson and countless dog lovers nationwide to pressure politicians to abolish greyhound racing in Arizona. In May 2016, Governor Doug Ducey signed bills ending live dog racing in the state. I was thrilled.

Tucson Greyhound Park's last live race after forty-four years came a month later. The place was rundown but stayed open, simulcasting races from other tracks. Hanke and I went there one night for reaction from fans during the last days of live racing. We counted the attendance on one hand. Five people were there. That's right, five. None were in the grandstand. They stood near television monitors, watching and betting on races from tracks around the world. There were more employees working the concession stands than there were attendees.

The track manager immediately kicked us out.

Social Insecurity

"I'll pay it forward. I promise."

—Reaction of a young man when hearing that a widow would pay off his debts

My most rewarding stories result in positive change for the community or an individual. One of those stories fell into my lap in 2017.

I received a call from a Tucson attorney named Joanne Hallinan. Joanne specializes in representing clients fighting the government in Social Security disability cases. She takes many cases pro bono because she cares about the less fortunate.

Joanne told me about a young man set on being a Marine, but his dream was in danger through no fault of his own. Jon Iniquez, a twenty-year-old Tucson resident, had wanted to serve his country since he was a kid. He showed us a photo of him dressed up as a Marine on Halloween when he was eleven.

Jon had been accepted to the Marines and was to report in a few months, but the Marines later told him he could not join until he paid off nearly $17,000 in debt. The debt was incurred by his parents because the Social Security Administration had overpaid their disability benefits. Both parents claimed Jon as a dependent, but only one could. They said it was an innocent mistake, that they never knew both were claiming him.

The military had a rule that a recruit's debt had to be less than 50 percent of his or her first-year salary. Jon would make $24,000 as a Marine, so he had to pay down $5,000 to meet that threshold. There was no way he could pay that by his reporting date. Jon was crushed.

"Some kids want to be rock stars or astronauts," he told me. "I've always wanted to be a Marine. People serve in different ways. And I just want to serve through the Marine Corps." I called the story "Social Insecurity."

The day after the report, I checked our Investigators Tip Line. There was a message from a viewer who said she wanted to pay off Jon's entire debt. I blurted out, "Holy shit." It was the kind of turn in a story that I lived for. Before I listened to the rest of the message, I yelled over to my photographer, "We have a follow-up on last night's piece." That was putting it mildly.

What a follow-up it was, thanks to an extraordinary viewer.

She was an eighty-year-old widow who wanted to remain anonymous, and for us to use only her first name, Judy. She said she didn't want or need publicity. We interviewed Judy in silhouette at her home in a Tucson retirement community. She said, "I wanted to do this because—don't make me cry—I feel sorry for people." She had no military connections, just kindness and charity in her heart.

"I don't like to see people suffer," she said. "I think if someone can get a chance at life and they're given a raw deal . . . I mean, this kid had a raw deal in life. You help people, you know? I'm not rich, but I can't take my money with me. I can do things like this."

I called Jon and told him. He was overwhelmed and grateful. He wanted to meet Judy, which I already had in mind, and Judy wanted to meet him. Jon came to her house with a big bouquet of flowers. Judy said, "I've got something for you, too." We shot the whole scene, again blurring her face as they met and hugged. She handed him a card with a check inside, for $17,000. Judy told him, "No strings. You just better turn out okay and pay back the world." Jon replied, "Wow. I'm just surprised and overwhelmed. If I can't pay it back, I'll pay it forward. I promise." Judy said, "That's what I meant."

After the interviews I drove home, and before I could get out of my car I received a phone call from the communications director for Representative (before she was appointed to the Senate) Martha McSally (R-Tucson). The staff member said McSally, an Air Force combat veteran, had seen our first report and her staff got Jon's Social Security debt waived. He could enlist as scheduled. I thought, *Can this story get any better?*

It was about to.

I immediately called Judy to tell her the debt was waived. She said Jon could keep the money. "I believe once you give a gift you never take it back," she said. "I just want him to pay it forward. He can use that money to start saving for his future."

I arranged a meeting between Jon and McSally. I did not tell Jon that Judy said he should keep her check. The meeting was at a local park, and when McSally approached Jon, she saluted him. They hugged for a long time and exchanged small talk. When I interviewed Jon on camera, I told him for the first time that Judy said he should keep the $17,000. He was silent for a few seconds. He blinked several times, swallowed hard, and said, "Wow. I don't know what to say. That's wonderful. I'm very grateful."

Jon reported for Marine duty on January 8, 2017. Judy, who had described herself as being spiritual, told me she believed that Jon's reporting date was no coincidence. Her husband, who died in 2009, would have been eighty-one on Jon's reporting date.

A fine young man received the justice he deserved. And to this day I keep in touch with Judy.

CHAPTER SIXTEEN

3 Gorillas

SOUND BITE:

"You're an investigative turd."

—Troy Emerson as he menacingly approached
me in the Pima County Superior Courthouse

I received a call in 2013 from a retired neurosurgeon who recently moved from his 6,000-square-foot Tucson home. Dr. Ron Bernstein claimed the moving company was holding his furniture and two expensive cars hostage in a billing dispute. This was the first time I heard of 3 Gorillas Moving & Storage and far from the last.

The company started moving hundreds of boxes out of Bernstein's home on January 13, 2013. Just four days later a Yamaha grand concert piano came up for auction on the online shopping site eBay. It was Bernstein's piano. The listed seller was the operations manager at 3 Gorillas.

We found the man who bought the piano, a public school music teacher named Ron Francis. He paid 3 Gorillas $14,250 for it, plus $750 for delivery. Francis saw Dr. Bernstein's name in paperwork that was in the piano's bench and contacted him. They became friends and Francis offered to sell the piano back, but Bernstein told him to keep it temporarily because he was going to Israel.

I called 3 Gorillas and requested an interview with owner Troy Emerson. He was supposedly a former boxer and looked it, with a muscular build and a cauliflower ear. I told him about Bernstein's claims. He said he would do an interview but wouldn't agree to a specific day and time.

The piece badly needed Emerson's responses on camera, but he stopped taking my calls. So a photographer and I went to the 3 Gorillas warehouse. We spotted Emerson driving a truck in front of it and followed him. He drove to a nearby fast-food place. We waited outside. We didn't want to disturb him during his lunch, or trespass.

When Emerson returned to his truck, I politely introduced myself, as I always did to interviewees. I gave Emerson all the specifics. He said 3 Gorillas had "every right" to auction off the piano because Bernstein hadn't paid him a dime. But I had the paperwork that showed Bernstein gave 3 Gorillas a $2,000 deposit on the first day of the move. Bernstein said he was told the move "wouldn't be more than $5,000." 3 Gorillas later sent Bernstein a bill for $31,000.

This is an extreme example of a huge problem in the moving business. I've heard of estimates being a couple thousand dollars too low, but in this case it was a $26,000 disparity. Many companies give low-ball estimates to get the job; then when the customer's stuff is on their truck, they say, "Sorry, you have a lot more furniture than we saw when we gave you the estimate, and you have to pay more before we deliver it." Lawmakers in many states, including Arizona, haven't regulated the moving business strongly enough.

After Emerson denied his company did anything wrong and claimed Bernstein was the culprit, he brought up Bernstein's religion. Bernstein is an Orthodox Jew. Emerson said he didn't want to attack Bernstein. "Hey, let's not get into this [criticizing Bernstein]. But one thing, I do love the Jewish people. So even if I had to donate thirty thousand dollars to this guy, I'd do it. Hey, I love the Jewish people," Emerson said.

I restrained a laugh when Emerson said that. The comment came so far out of left field. I put it in the piece. Sometimes you use comments that may seem irrelevant but show a side of someone. It was the first time I'd ever heard a businessman I was investigating bring up religion like that. It reminded me of the awful, old, racist line "Hey, some of my best friends are black." I can't be sure, but I think Emerson knew that I'm Jewish (with a name like Schwartz). It felt like he was patronizing me. Maybe he naïvely believed that because he "loved the Jewish people" it would affect how I wrote the story.

After the interview, as my photographer and I walked away, Emerson yelled, "Say hi to Bill for me."

Bill Shaw was the general manager at KVOA. I knew Emerson was trying to let me know he was friendly with my boss, as if that, too, would affect me. I played dumb. I turned around and yelled back to Emerson, "Bill who?"

I then researched 3 Gorillas history. I found out the company had an "F" rating with the Better Business Bureau and was the target of more complaints to the BBB than any other mover in Southern Arizona. That said a lot, because so many people complain about moving companies. I got the names of the customers who complained about 3 Gorillas.

One of them was a woman named Karen Barbera. She said when 3 Gorillas moved her family from Oro Valley, Arizona, to North Tustin, California, in 2012, the original estimate was $15,000. She showed me the final bill. It was for $38,000.

Barbera said, "When I contested it they said, 'Listen, if you want to cause trouble, we'll put all of your furniture out on the sidewalk.'" She said 3 Gorillas movers scratched the hardwood floors in her new home and showed me photos of the scratches. She said the movers also damaged and lost numerous items. Her insurance company later agreed, listing twenty-two lost items totaling almost $11,000.

My first report on 3 Gorillas aired January 30, 2014, on KVOA's 10 p.m. news. When I arrived at work the following day, my phone's light was flashing with twelve messages. They were all about the report. I also had twenty-seven emails about it. None of the messages were from satisfied customers. And a few came from former employees.

Chris Gillam said he was a mover and driver for 3 Gorillas on and off for ten years. In a report that aired three weeks after the first one, Gillam alleged that the company had been "ripping off customers for years." He said it was "standard practice" that "they low-ball a job." "They call it a good-faith estimate," he said sarcastically. Gillam claimed that once the company had a customer's furniture on their truck, "they would double or triple the cost of the move." He said if packing was involved in a particular move, the company would add on packing that never happened. "Say they used five dish packs, they'll put down ten. Or if they used four mirror cartons, they'll put seven or eight down. They paid the bill," Gillam alleged.

Gillam claimed if a Tucson resident was moving to the Phoenix area 115 miles away, 3 Gorillas would "add like a $600 flat rate travel charge. They don't tell the customer that until after the stuff is on the truck."

Gillam said he was fired a month earlier after accusing Emerson of shorting his paycheck. I asked Gillam, "Why should people believe you, a disgruntled employee who got fired?" He replied, "I say, look at the facts." He showed us paychecks that indicated he was indeed not fully paid for the hours he worked.

I asked Gillam what he knew about the dispute between the company and Dr. Bernstein, since Gillam was employed by 3 Gorillas during Bernstein's move. He said, "Oh, they bragged about it in the office." He also said Bernstein's stereo system was not in warehouse storage with the rest of his stuff, but in the company office. Gillam claimed employees played music on it and joked about it. I later obtained a photo of the stereo inside the office and showed it on the air.

I called Emerson and he said I needed to talk to his wife because she handled paychecks; then he hung up on me. I went to the 3

Gorillas office. His wife kicked me out and said, "Don't you come back here."

Dr. Bernstein sued 3 Gorillas. We covered every day of the two-week trial. The jury awarded him $1.7 million. Emerson did not talk to me during or after the trial. He did give me dirty looks when we passed in the hallway. A couple of years later while I was in the courthouse for jury duty he approached and called me an "investigative turd." I thought it was original. He then walked menacingly towards me. His attorney pulled him away.

Around the time of the Bernstein trial, several more 3 Gorillas customers filed complaints with the Arizona attorney general. The AG filed a consumer fraud suit against 3 Gorillas. After a bench trial, the judge found that Emerson and his company violated the Consumer Fraud Act and had "misrepresented to some customers that 3 Gorillas was affiliated with a national moving company"; that it "failed to address some consumer claims after personal property had been damaged during the move"; and "misrepresented prices quoted to consumers, and then told a consumer they would not leave the consumer's home unless a new, higher price was paid or did not deliver a consumer's belongings because the new, higher price was not paid."

The judge concluded that "3 Gorillas and Emerson engaged in deceptive practices, misrepresentations, and suppressed or omitted material facts in connection with the sale or advertisement of services." The court further banned 3 Gorillas and Emerson from "engaging in deceptive, unfair and fraudulent business practices" and ordered the company to pay a total of $17,010 in restitution to seven consumers. The company was also ordered to pay a civil penalty fine of $18,000 and the state's attorney fees and costs.

I went to 3 Gorillas' office a second time for reaction. Emerson's wife, Lyn Bernabe, called sheriff's deputies. They met with her for about a half hour, and Bernabe showed them the web version of my previous story in which she told me, "Don't you ever come back here."

The deputies emerged from the moving office and arrested me for trespassing. They said they had to because Bernabe previously told me not to return.

I wasn't handcuffed, just given the arrest papers and told to report to court in a few weeks. KVOA's brilliant attorney, Peter Limperis, met with 3 Gorillas' lawyer. Limperis told him if the case went to trial, he would show the judge the many stories I had done on 3 Gorillas over the past year, with all the angry former customers. 3 Gorillas dropped the trespassing charge.

Over several months after my initial stories on 3 Gorillas, I received phone calls from forty-two former employees of another moving company in Tucson called Assurance Relocation Systems. The callers worked there mostly as drivers and movers. But a couple worked in the office, and one call came from a manager of a staffing agency. All said the same thing, that Assurance Relocation Systems didn't pay them for work they performed. The Assurance Relocation Systems owner was Lyn Bernabe, Troy Emerson's wife. Emerson worked there because 3 Gorillas apparently wasn't getting much business anymore.

The former workers at Assurance said Bernabe made up excuses for why she hadn't paid them, usually claiming they stole or damaged equipment. One former employee was a very believable nineteen-year-old part-time college student. He gave me undercover video of Bernabe cursing at him and accusing him of stealing a moving dolly, which he strongly denied. He said, "Why would I need a dolly? Why would I risk my job for something I don't need?"

A spokesperson for the Industrial Commission of Arizona said ninety-three former employees of Assurance Relocation Systems filed wage claims with the state and most won. The former workers told me Bernabe still didn't pay them. So the amounts they were owed had tripled. When I called Bernabe, a man hung up on me when I asked about the accusations. It was Troy Emerson.

I learned that Assurance Relocation Systems got a good portion of its business from the Air Force. Tucson is home to Davis-Monthan Air Force Base. Some of the complaints I received came from airmen.

Many former workers also filed complaints with the Arizona attorney general's office. A spokesperson for the attorney general told me the AG's office "is reviewing the case" against Assurance Relocation Systems. Not one employee who won a wage claim told me they got paid, almost a year after their paychecks were due.

CHAPTER SEVENTEEN

Wrongful Withdrawal

SOUND BITE:

"I know when my husband died. He was home. I was taking care of him. I was there when he took his last breath."

—Virginia McGee, on a costly mistake made by the Veterans Administration

V eterans administration hospitals around the country have been the target of countless complaints for being inept, uncaring, and providing poor treatment to patients. I received a call in May 2017 from a woman who claimed the VA would not correct a mistake that was causing her financial problems.

Virginia McGee of Sierra Vista, Arizona, told me she had been fighting the Tucson VA for two months and asked for my help. She told me about her husband, Dana, a twenty-year Army veteran. He was a crew chief on Mohawk aircraft and a recipient of the Meritorious Service Medal. Virginia was also an Army vet and that's how they met. They were married for thirty-six years and had two sons.

Virginia said Dana was loving and sensitive on the inside, tough on the outside. "I never saw him cry except when a kitten was dying," she said through tears.

Dana retired from the Army in 1995. Due to severe knee problems he received a disability benefit of $263 a month. He developed dementia and died on Friday the thirteenth of January 2017 at age fifty-nine. "I told him I wasn't ready for him to go," Virginia said. "I needed him to stay." She was a widow at fifty-eight.

Her personal loss was followed by a financial loss.

Two months after Dana died, Virginia received a letter from her credit union. It informed her that the VA had withdrawn $3,159 from the account she and her husband had shared. "I was shocked," she said about the withdrawal. She had no idea what it was for. She said when she first read it, she was thinking, "Are you kidding me? As if I don't have enough to deal with? My husband's gone and you're going to violate my savings account?"

Here's the mistake the VA made: it recorded Dana's death as January 13, 2016. Virginia said he died a year later, and showed me the death certificate. It showed that he did indeed pass away on January 13, 2017.

One incorrect digit led the VA to believe it overpaid Dana a year's worth of benefits.

"I know when my husband died," she said. "He was home. I was taking care of him. I was there when he took his last breath."

She said immediately after she received the letter about the withdrawal, she called the VA and the agency admitted the mistake. But two months later it still hadn't put the money back in her account. That's why she called us. "They shouldn't have taken it out in the first place," she said. "All they had to do was eyeball the death certificate. They had it right there on his account."

We called the VA after getting off the phone with Mrs. McGee. A day later, a spokesperson said the refund was being processed and would be in her account in seven to ten days. The money was refunded the day after I called a VA media relations spokesman.

"I don't think it would have happened if you hadn't come here," Virginia said to me.

A VA spokesperson confirmed the mistake and told me, "It was a clerical error."

The VA spokesman continued, "When Mrs.McGee called to report his passing, the call center representative wrote down the wrong year. He entered 2016 instead of 2017."

It might have been an innocent mistake, a simple clerical error. But there's no way it should've taken two months to fix it. And people wonder why some VA offices have a bad name.

Mrs. McGee said she would have appreciated a letter or call from the VA before the money was taken out of her account. She hoped our story would cause VA employees to pay more attention when recording important case notes.

Not only did stories like this feel incredibly rewarding, they prompted other viewers in need of help to contact me about their problems with the VA. Thankfully, I haven't heard from a viewer who had a wrongful withdrawal since Mrs. McGee's story.

CHAPTER EIGHTEEN

Dental Disaster

SOUND BITE:

"I don't know whether I want to cry or kill them. They left me with no teeth."

—Tucson resident Lyn Millard, after her dentist's office closed without telling her

L yn Millard saved all the money she had, $4,000, to get much-needed dental implants. A dentist at a practice called Half Dental did only half the job.

He pulled her bottom teeth in preparation for the implants; then the office suddenly closed. Lyn was sixty-two and disabled, the result of being hit by a car while riding her bicycle. She lived alone, on $930 a month. When Lyn called me in July 2018, she had no money and no bottom teeth.

The chain of Half Dental offices had been plagued by lawsuits filed by its owners and franchisees before all ten of its offices nationwide closed. That left Lyn and many other patients around the country with unfinished dental work. The dentist who left Lyn in mid-treatment was practicing in another state when I did the story and didn't return my calls. He was not disciplined by the Arizona State

Board of Dental Examiners for abandoning Lyn. I called a couple of dentists I knew, and they called the board's inaction "unbelievable." The Board of Dental Examiners declined comment.

From my experience dealing with dental and medical boards in several states, the inaction wasn't surprising. They tend to bend over backwards for their dentists and doctors. It seemed to me these health professionals almost had to kill a patient for the board to discipline them.

Lyn said due to her dental disaster, "I can't chew, I can't smile correctly." She opened her mouth wide on camera and showed her bottom gums.

Minutes after our report aired, I received a phone call that was in line with my job to help the helpless. Or, in this case, give teeth to the toothless.

Dr. Robert Wood was the co-owner of Arizona Oral Surgeons and Maxillofacial Surgeons. He offered to treat Lyn for free. He typically charged $6,000 for this treatment.

I arranged for Lyn to meet Dr. Wood at his office. My first question to Wood was the obvious one, "Why are you doing this for free?"

He said, "It's good karma. I think everyone in this world, including every one of us, at some time needs help, and I think it's the right thing to do to reach out and help people."

Lyn said, "It's just wonderful. I'm overwhelmed. That kind of money, to give me teeth, you know? It's amazing."

Regarding Half Dental splitting town unannounced and not refunding Lyn, Dr. Wood said, "It's not ethical and it really isn't legal as well. I mean, people that close their practice have an obligation to see that those patients are referred, so that they can receive the appropriate care."

Another Tucson dentist named Rodney Gold also contacted me after watching the report. He said he'd make Lyn a new lower denture and do related work for free. He would usually charge $2,700 for that. Four other dentists also offered free treatment, but Lyn was all set with the first two who reached out to us. I mentioned all the dentists' names on the air. In many cases I didn't provide free publicity for companies I thought could buy a commercial. But I thought these dentists deserved mention.

Dr. Wood said, "Sometimes you need to step in and do that and make things right. That's kind of a duty to the profession. I and my other surgical colleagues in town have all done the same thing."

Doctors Wood and Gold told me that Lyn's new teeth would be ready a couple of months later, around Thanksgiving Day. *What a nice holiday story*, I thought, and told them to contact me a few days earlier so we could schedule the follow-up piece.

Two months before Thanksgiving I received a call from Dr. Wood's office. Lyn Millard was found dead in her home. The medical examiner said it was a heart attack.

Until now, I told no one about Lyn's death except my photographer. I didn't see any reason to put it on the air. She wasn't a celebrity or public person. I thought announcing her passing would be an invasion of privacy for her survivors. And how would I write it? *Remember that woman we helped get free dental treatment? She died.* Sometimes you just make decisions you feel are correct. I had no precedent; I just felt it was the right call.

CHAPTER NINETEEN

Dirty Detective

SOUND BITE:

"I know it looks bad, but I had no reason to ever take anybody's stuff."

—Detective David Tarnow, while under investigation
by his own department for stealing homeowners' jewelry

S ome investigative stories are layups. Someone gives you all the proof you need, and after you confirm everything, all you have to do is get the necessary elements—video, relevant documents, and the interviews. Some investigative stories start off simple but get more complex as you peel back layers of information. A piece I first did in August 2015 started as a layup, but the depth of it and its consequences turned it into a more difficult shot.

A guy who felt he was being badgered by members of the Pima County Sheriff's Department called me and said he had damning information about a detective. The tipster said he would not go on camera, even with his face covered, but would give me the information. I met regularly with tipsters without a camera if they had a possible story, especially with those who said they had proof. All I had to lose was a little time.

I agreed to meet with this guy at the station without a camera. The tipster sure did have damning information—an audio recording of an internal affairs detective interviewing a fellow detective under investigation for theft. This was extraordinary. It was the first time I had audio of an internal affairs interview. The interviewee was David Tarnow, a fifty-six-year-old burglary unit detective with fifteen years on the job.

The informant said Tarnow was being investigated because he pawned stolen items recovered from burglaries and kept the money. The investigation began three months earlier when a burglary victim filed a complaint against Tarnow. The victim owned an expensive home in the upscale Foothills section of Tucson. More than $1 million worth of jewelry and artwork was stolen from the man's house in 2011. Tanow was sent to investigate.

The homeowner alleged that he and Tarnow went together to several pawn shops, hoping to find his stolen items. According to the victim, the pair found a lot of his stuff in the shops. But instead of Tarnow getting them back to the homeowner, he told him he needed to do a lot of paperwork to recover the items from the shops, and it would take time. According to the tipster, Tarnow then went back to the pawn shops—alone—told the shop owners he was a detective and took the stolen items without ever telling the victim.

The tipster gave us numerous pawn shop transaction slips with Detective Tarnow's name on them as the seller. The slips showed Tarnow received $2,700 for two gold bracelets, over $1,000 for a gold coin, and profits from other hot items.

The tipster obviously had help from someone inside the sheriff's department to obtain the internal affairs audio and the pawn shop slips. Someone in the department wanted this story to come out.

Sheriff's department investigators also were looking into whether Tarnow took jewelry from the department's property room, sold it, and replaced it with cheap costume jewelry. The officers are supposed to leave detailed descriptions of what they take out of the room, even if for a minute. But Tarnow left vague, hard-to-read descriptions because he allegedly replaced the stolen items with cheap replacements. He hoped no one would notice the difference.

I spent hours digesting the documents the tipster provided, then called the sheriff. He arranged an off-camera meeting with the investigators on the Tarnow case. I brought a photographer because I wanted him to learn the details. I always thought it was helpful for a photographer to know as much as possible about a story before shooting it, so he or she could also think about the video we would need.

We were escorted to the meeting room at the county sheriff's department. There were three detectives seated around a long conference table. This was obviously a significant investigation. They were colleagues of Tarnow's from the burglary squad, including his supervisor, and a public information officer who served as the liaison to the news media.

The head of the burglary unit made it clear at the start that the information under discussion was on background. They asked me to hold the story until they were closer to an arrest. I said that would be fine. I didn't want to jeopardize the case. But I told them they first needed to confirm if the facts and documents presented to me by the tipster were accurate. Since they came from a street hustler with a grudge against Tarnow specifically and cops in general, I needed official confirmation.

They confirmed everything.

They also added even more damning allegations against Tarnow. They told me he resigned a few days earlier, and when a colleague cleaned out his desk, he found a box full of jewelry that Tarnow had allegedly stolen.

The tipster had told me that before the victim of the big Foothills burglary became suspicious about Tarnow pawning his stuff, Tarnow had asked him for a loan of $12,000 in cash. I never heard of a cop borrowing money from a victim of a crime he was investigating. This was bizarre. While not illegal, it was certainly unethical. Sheriff Nanos said, "It's a conflict of interest, clearly. We just don't do that, and I mean there's just certain things that common sense tells you don't do."

My first report—called "Dirty Detective?"—aired on August 11, 2015. I didn't name Tarnow because station management had a policy of not identifying anyone until he or she was officially charged. The highlight of the story was the audio from the IA interrogation. Here's part of it:

> **IA investigator:** "You know what, man? I'm not going to beat around the bush or anything."
> **Tarnow:** "That's fine."
> **Investigator:** "The reason I brought you here was because, looking at everything, it's pretty suspicious."
> **Tarnow:** "It is."
> **Investigator:** "You're aware of that."
> **Tarnow:** "Yeah."
> **Investigator:** "You know, all this stuff."
> **Tarnow:** "I know it looks bad, but I had no reason to ever take anybody's stuff."
>
> Then the interrogator focused on the complaint from the victim in the 2011 burglary.
>
> **Investigator:** "Did you take anything?"
> **Tarnow:** "I did not take a thing from him."
> **Investigator:** "Did you take anything from anybody?"
> **Tarnow:** "No."

During my interview with Sheriff Nanos, I asked, "Should burglary victims watching this think that maybe this detective sold their stuff?" He said, "Well, absolutely. I mean if he was assigned to their case, yeah. . . . I have that concern, so I would hope they have that concern."

I showed Tarnow's property room sign-out slips with the almost illegible handwriting to Nanos. He said, "That's very nondescript. That's sloppy work. That's not tolerated."

I went to Tarnow's home to see if he would talk. We would hide his face if he asked us to because he hadn't been charged at this point. I heard someone inside his home, but no one answered the door. I left my business card with a note to please call me.

The next day, Tarnow called. I was surprised, because from my experience cops under investigation rarely call reporters. They might have their attorney call, and usually the lawyer will say something like, "My client is innocent and I will prove that in court, not through the news media."

Tarnow told me, "They can investigate me all they want. They're not going to find anything. I haven't done anything wrong." I asked about the box full of jewelry investigators said they found in his desk. He said, "That's not true. I handed it to my supervisor the day I resigned." I asked him for an on-camera interview with or without his face shown. He declined, but what he told me was on the record, and I reported it.

Five months later, Tarnow was indicted on three counts of trafficking in stolen property, two counts of fraud and one count each of theft and extortion. He later changed his plea to guilty to the fraud charge. The judge did not allow our camera in court at Tarnow's sentencing. Tarnow was going to prison and the judge said he could be a target for other inmates because he was a cop. But by that time, Tarnow's mug shot had been on all the Tucson television stations and in the newspaper. Before the sentencing we waited for Tarnow outside the courthouse and tried to interview him. He was pacing back and forth, smoking a cigarette. I walked up to him with our camera rolling and asked, "Mr. Tarnow, would you like to say anything?" He replied, "Nothing."

I received one angry email from a viewer (apparently a friend of Tarnow) who thought I was wrong for approaching him. I replied that he was a former detective who violated his oath, and I thought maybe he would want to say something to the public, maybe show some remorse. Remember, even when he was questioned by investigators in his own department, Tarnow lied about stealing anything and lied to me on the phone. I told the viewer it was my job to approach Tarnow, at the only opportunity I had since the case broke.

Tarnow was sentenced to four and a half years in prison

CHAPTER TWENTY

Abandoned Baby

SOUND BITE:

"If they had awards for the worst mother ever, Marina Garcia has to be a strong competitor for winner."

—Richard Wintory, the attorney for Marina Garcia's ex-husband

A bizarre story in the Sierra Vista News in 2018 grabbed my attention. I generally didn't report stories published elsewhere unless I could advance it or get an important missing element. This story didn't have an interview with the key person, so I saw an opportunity.

Marina Garcia was the thirty-one-year-old wife of an Army sergeant stationed in South Korea. She got pregnant shortly before her twenty-four-year-old husband was deployed. Steven Garcia told me via a Skype interview that he was overjoyed about becoming a father.

Marina gave birth to a healthy boy while Steven was overseas. But she told Steven's family the child died during birth. Steven was devastated.

It was a lie. The baby was fine.

And Steven wasn't the father.

Marina gave the infant to a married couple she was old friends with and didn't tell anyone. She simply gave her baby away.

Alex and Leslie Hernandez lived in Texas and were driving back there from Sierra Vista when an Arizona state trooper pulled them over. Alex was doing ninety in a seventy-mile-per-hour zone. The trooper saw a three-day-old baby in the car and asked the couple about him.

Alex and Leslie told investigators the truth. They said Marina gave them the baby to raise as their own because she felt overwhelmed and couldn't handle being a mother.

Sources told me Marina had a history of getting married to soldiers with good benefits, and she didn't work.

After I had these previously unreported facts about the case, I found an address for Marina at an apartment complex in Sierra Vista. I knocked on the door with a photographer rolling. A man dressed in Army fatigues answered. I gave him my card and told him I'd like to talk to Marina. He told me to wait and closed the door. We heard talking from inside the apartment.

I was surprised when after about five minutes, Marina came outside.

"Hi, I'm Matthew Schwartz from KVOA," I said in my usual friendly way.

Marina replied in an angry tone, "I know who you are." I found it kind of funny that she appeared angry but also wanted to talk.

Marina denied doing anything wrong, even giving the child to friends. She said the truth would come out in court.

By this time, Steven had told me that although the baby wasn't his, he wanted to adopt him and raise him as his own. Steven himself was adopted and said his adoptive parents made him the solid citizen he had become. I told Marina that Steven was seeking custody.

"He's not gonna get custody of the baby. He's not the biological father," she said.

That much was true, according to DNA tests. I asked her, "Will you tell us who is?"

"Uh, it's an unknown. It's unknown," she said.

A source later told me the baby was the product of a very brief relationship Marina had with a man she met at a bar in Colorado.

Also unknown was why Marina had become so angry with Steven. The couple was recently married. They had dated for only two months.

She changed her mind about her innocence when prosecutors got the Hernandez couple to testify against her. I was the only reporter in the courtroom when Marina pleaded guilty to attempted scheme to defraud, a felony. This story had received some national play, so I was somewhat surprised no other reporters were there. It was another example of a good story not being followed up by news outlets. When I asked Marina on the way into court for a comment, she ignored me and kept walking.

Cochise county judge John Kelliher wouldn't let us show Marina's face because she had received death threats on social media. He told Marina that she could have given up the child for adoption while in the hospital. She claimed she wasn't aware she could do that.

When it came Marina's turn to speak, she was hyperventilating and crying. She couldn't talk for a full minute. She said she accepted full responsibility and should have done things differently.

The judge asked her, "The question is would you do things differently because you got caught?"

Her lawyer said, "I don't believe this is an individual that needs to be incarcerated. She has taken responsibility."

The judge held back tears himself at times. I had never seen a judge so emotional. He lectured Garcia.

"You compounded your lies. You made that snowball going down the hill incredibly large. It shocks the conscience because we're dealing with another human being, a child. But also a father," Kelliher said.

Marina was sentenced to four months in jail and five years probation. The prosecutor said, "I think that the message is if you want to give your baby up for adoption that you should go through the legal process and do it the right way."

In October 2019 I received a tip that there was a felony warrant out for Marina's arrest. After serving her jail time, she failed to show up for a restitution hearing and a meeting with her probation officer. Her whereabouts were unknown. Like other criminals I covered, Marina Garcia went from being repentant to again skirting the law.

Marina was arrested in December 2019 in a store in Sierra Vista. She was awaiting sentencing for violating probation at the time of this writing.

Steven Garcia divorced Marina and was granted sole custody of the baby. He transferred to an Army base in the US and was taking care of the infant with his parents' help.

CHAPTER TWENTY-ONE

Here Comes the Judge

SOUND BITE:

"As far as I know, I'm going to get an award from the attorney general's office."

—Anne Segal, a Pima County justice of the peace, when asked why she had been summoned to the Arizona attorney general's office for a meeting

A 2014 republican primary for Pima County justice of the peace was a bitter campaign. Magistrates, as they are also called, preside over civil lawsuits involving disputes in amounts of $10,000 or lower. They include drunk-driving cases, landlord-tenant disputes, and writing bad checks.

About a month before the primary, two independent sources told me the incumbent candidate was under investigation by the Arizona attorney general. The state's most powerful lawyer wanted to talk to Judge Anne Segal. The sixty-one-year-old Tucson resident allegedly was not following sentencing guidelines in some bad-check cases. Segal was supposedly doling out lesser sentences than the law mandated.

I contacted the court administrator to confirm the tip. He emailed me that not only was it true that Segal was under an investigation by the AG, but that he learned this from Segal herself. Administrator Doug Kooi sent me an email saying, "Judge Segal made me aware that the Attorney General's Office is conducting an investigation related to some cases that were heard in her courtroom. She will be meeting with them sometime in August."

The meeting was scheduled for after the primary, and I thought voters needed to know that a candidate was under investigation *before* they cast their ballots. A sitting judge was being investigated by the attorney general, a judge whose annual salary of $101,500 came from taxpayers' dollars.

After confirming the investigation, I called Judge Segal. She said she did receive a phone call from the AG investigator, but denied she was under investigation. She said she didn't want to discuss it but would give me an interview in November, after the general election. *Too late*, I thought.

I called a source who told me Segal had a public forum scheduled the following evening at a local library. I told my news director that I needed to be there with a photographer to question the judge, and she agreed.

I thought if I approached Segal away from the audience at her event, she might be more willing to answer my questions. I told my photographer to wait outside the library while I went to the room where Segal's talk was being held. Segal, her husband, and their daughter were there. Segal cancelled the event because no one showed up.

I went outside and told my photographer to come in. When I questioned the judge, she denied being under investigation and telling the court administrator that she was. She began walking through the library to the exit. I walked with her and we had this exchange:

Me: "I was told by the administrator of the court that you told him that you're being investigated."

Segal: "And I'm telling you I'm not being investigated. My opponent cannot afford to make publicity, cannot afford TV. So this is a good way to get an adverse spot."

Me: "But Doug Kooi told me this. He's the court administrator; he's not your opponent. Why would he tell me this?"

Segal: "I have no idea why he would tell you that. I am not being investigated by the attorney general's office. You're making up news that isn't there. I don't know what you're saying. I don't know what you're talking about."

Me: "You told me yesterday on the phone that you did receive a phone call from an investigator in the attorney general's office. You said that on the phone to me."

Segal: "I don't know who the gentleman . . . I don't know . . . no. I don't know anything you're talking about."

Me: "Yesterday you did tell me, Judge, that it was an investigator."

Segal: "I don't know what you're talking about. Well, I received a phone call that said there was an anonymous inquiry about anonymous papers. I have no idea what it's about."

The day after the piece ran, here came the judge. Segal read the riot act to my boss, KVOA news director Cathie Batbie. I always let Cathie know about planned confrontations so she would not be surprised by an angry phone call from the interviewee or his or her attorney. Segal's call to Cathie was an angry one.

Most importantly to me, Segal didn't say anything in the story was inaccurate. She said she was unprepared and caught off guard. I think the real reason she called was because she looked bad shortly before the primary and knew it. I told my boss, "How could she be caught off guard? I called Judge Segal the day before I confronted her. She had to know when she saw me at the library what I was going to ask her." Cathie said Segal requested another interview, and said she'd do it with Cathie but not me. Cathie agreed, but I protested. I speculated that management wanted to appease someone it viewed as a VIP.

Management at all media outlets should never let an outsider dictate who should conduct an interview. I thought management should have told Segal, "This is Schwartz's story. You either do the follow-up with him or no one." At the very least, another reporter could do the follow-up. It was a journalistic issue—not an ego thing.

I wanted the station to report in the follow-up that Segal refused to talk to me for the piece. I didn't want to become part of the story, but Segal, by declining to talk to me, had injected me into it. I lost that battle as well.

While I was stewing, the station's attorney and I gave my news director questions she needed to ask the judge.

During the follow-up Segal criticized my conduct during the library confrontation. She said I was "yelling," that I "interfered" with her meeting and "made children cry in the library."

Again, there was no one at the meeting other than Segal's husband and daughter. When Segal was asked by my boss about my supposed conduct, she backtracked. "I probably overstated it," she said. "He caught me unprepared."

Here is the key part of the exchange from the follow-up:

> **KVOA:** "You're telling us that Doug Kooi [court administrator] did not tell us the truth in that email?"
> **Segal:** "I guess I have to say that he didn't tell you the truth because I'm not being investigated."

KVOA: "You haven't talked to Mr. Kooi at all about his statement to us?"

Segal: "No, no, I really haven't. I take that back. No, I take that back. I talked to Mr. Kooi, I spoke to Doug Kooi. I told him I got a phone call. That's what he knows. That's what I know. I received a phone call that said there was an anonymous inquiry about anonymous paper. I have no idea what it's about."

KVOA: "So you didn't ask them what this inquiry was about?"

Segal: "No."

KVOA: "What kinds of questions they needed the answers to?"

Segal: "No. We set a meeting up in September. It's back burner. It's not of interest."

However, the voters apparently were interested. Segal got trounced in the primary and was later censured by the Arizona Supreme Court and reprimanded by the Arizona Commission on Judicial Conduct. In its report the commission found, and Segal agreed, that she "made false and misleading statements to KVOA, News 4 Tucson" and that she knew about the AG's investigation into some of her rulings. The commission said Segal "recklessly misrepresented" the facts.

When Segal left the bench on December 31, 2014, she had five public reprimands and one censure (a censure is more serious than a reprimand). According to the Commission on Judicial Conduct, the six public sanctions were the most ever against any judge in the state. There was no punishment levied against Segal because by the time the investigation ended, there were only days left in her term on the bench.

Segal went into private practice and lost another bid for justice of the peace in 2018. That year I was hosting a charity event. There were twenty tables there and Segal was at the one next to me. Tucson is a small town and stuff like this happens. Segal approached me and could not have been nicer. She said nothing about the story four years earlier, and neither did I.

CHAPTER TWENTY-TWO

A Woman's Outrage (and mine)

SOUND BITE:

"I'm here to tell my story. I'm here to help others, and I've lost two years of my life so far."

—Melissa Triano Gee, who accused a powerful university dean of raping her

News organizations typically do not identify victims or alleged victims of sex crimes. However, a woman who said she was drugged and raped by a former dean at the University of Arizona told me in 2017 that she no longer wanted to remain anonymous. She said she wanted to do an interview showing her face and using her name. It had been two years since the alleged incident, which was headline news in Tucson.

Melissa Triano alleged that she had been sexually assaulted by Jesse Lyle Bootman, the dean of the College of Pharmacy at the University of Arizona for twenty-eight years. According to his Bloomberg profile, Bootman was consistently picked as one of the fifty most influential pharmacists in America by *American Druggist.*

Melissa was often emotional recounting on camera the night of the alleged assault. She said, "I've been numb, suicidal. At times, completely heartbroken."

I too became heartbroken—and furious—when KVOA killed the story. Here's the background:

Melissa and Bootman were old acquaintances. They ran into each other one night at a restaurant. Bootman was sixty-seven; she was forty-seven at the time. She was engaged and moving in with her fiancé the next day. She said Bootman bought her and her girlfriend a drink and told them about a great house he recently bought. Melissa was a real estate agent and had a real estate photography business. She said Bootman asked if she would like to see his house.

"I went [to Bootman's home] because he invited me to see it and I was being polite," Melissa told me. "I considered him a friend. Someone I had no reason to fear. It was nearby, so I went on my way home. I was not afraid of him. Obviously, I never considered being drugged to a point [where] I couldn't defend myself or leave."

Melissa claimed that shortly after they arrived at Bootman's home, he gave her a drink. The next thing she said she remembered was waking up the following morning in bed next to him. She was bloody and bruised. She said a dildo was near the bed.

"My lip was bleeding, my nose was broken. I was having trouble walking. My leg hurt. And I was frightened," she said.

According to Melissa, Bootman claimed she tripped and fell during the night. When she asked him about the dildo, she said he told her she had complained about having a sore back and that he rubbed it with the sex toy.

Melissa went to a hospital. According to the Pima County Sheriff's Department report, a nurse called her vaginal injuries "the worst I have ever seen."

Lab reports I obtained showed a common date-rape drug was in Melissa's system, and her DNA was on the bedsheets and the sex toy.

Melissa called Bootman the day after the alleged attack, with a detective from the sheriff's department listening (a "confrontation call"). Bootman said they did not have sex. When later confronted with the results of the DNA, Bootman said they *did* have sex that night, but that it was consensual.

Bootman always maintained his innocence of the charges against him. The case was moved to Maricopa County at the request of Bootman's lawyers, who claimed Pima County investigators were biased towards Melissa because they knew her from a previous, unrelated murder case. Melissa's uncle Gary Triano was killed in an infamous incident that got national attention in 1996 when a pipe bomb planted in his car exploded. His former wife, Pam Phillips, was convicted nearly eighteen years later of hiring a hit man. She was sentenced to life in prison.

Melissa and her lawyer felt the change of venue was a terrible, unnecessary move by Pima county attorney Barbara LaWall. Melissa said the only two investigators she knew from her uncle's murder were retired. The change of venue was a victory for Bootman because the case had received so much publicity in Pima County, implying he could not get a fair trial there.

In October 2017, almost exactly two years after the alleged sexual attack, Maricopa county attorney Bill Montgomery dismissed all criminal charges against Bootman. Montgomery declined an interview. He sent an email saying he had doubts about the chance of obtaining a conviction. "Questions surrounding the nature of prior interactions between the victim and the defendant and the circumstances surrounding the allegations of a sexual assault cannot be satisfactorily addressed at this point in time with the available evidence," the statement read.

Montgomery apparently was referring to the weekend in 2011 that Melissa spent in a condominium Bootman owned in San Diego. Melissa told me she had just declared bankruptcy, was unemployed, and needed a break when she stayed there. She said she was there alone.

However, Bootman's lawyers filed court documents that showed she and Bootman planned to meet up and stay at his condo together. The documents said Bootman bought both of their airline tickets. His attorneys said the two were lovers who "spent the night" in a "romantic relationship." Melissa said the two were never romantically involved or had intimate relations.

Melissa did the interview with me days after the dismissal. (She had gotten married since the alleged attack and her name was Melissa Triano Gee.) She said on camera, "I'm heartbroken that our elected officials have allowed this to happen. I think they should be ashamed of themselves."

The interview ended with Melissa saying, "I believe in God. And I believe that the truth will always come out in the end."

Management at KVOA was afraid Bootman might sue the station because the criminal charges against him were dismissed. (The charges were dismissed "without prejudice," meaning they could be brought again.)

I disagreed strongly about the interview being killed. I used only facts that were in court or police records and attributed all material used in the story. I attempted to be balanced, asking Bootman for an interview. He declined through his attorney, but my script included a long statement from his lawyer proclaiming Bootman's innocence. I did not see anything defamatory in the script. While I strongly disagreed with management's decision on this story, the station's general manager, Bill Shaw, did allow me to do other stories that were potentially litigious and cost the station advertising dollars. Many GMs in small markets would not have the guts to allow me to report such stories.

There was also a civil suit filed by Melissa related to the alleged attack. That suit was pending when management didn't run the interview with Melissa. My news director told me the story was not actually killed, but "put on hold" pending the outcome of the civil case.

I didn't believe it would ever air, and it didn't.

Seven months later, a settlement was reached in the civil case. The amount of money involved was not disclosed. Melissa's attorney said, "All I can tell you is the case has been settled to our satisfaction."

I did another interview with Melissa two years later, in April 2019. This report *was* approved by management because it didn't focus on the alleged attack. Melissa had sued Bootman's original lawyer for defamation and won, and the story was about that case. The defamation suit was prompted by something Bootman's first attorney said about Melissa during a news conference three weeks after the 2015 incident. He said, "She hired two attorneys within days of making this complaint, which reflects her financial motivations. She has a significant criminal history and a history of financial problems."

Melissa said in our 2019 interview, "I was crushed" about those comments and "they were not true." I researched her background and found the 2010 bankruptcy she had previously told me about. The records showed she had no significant criminal history.

The jury in the defamation case found Bootman's original lawyer had defamed Melissa. She was awarded $25,000. A prominent lawyer I interviewed said, "I don't know of a case like that in the United States." Melissa's attorney, Bill Walker, said, "I think this case will have a huge significance. Now, criminal defense lawyers are going to know that they may have to pay the piper if they lie about the victim."

CHAPTER TWENTY-THREE

Tainted Justice?

SOUND BITE:

"It's a huge deal and all I need to prove that is put yourself in one of our clients' positions. You're arrested, you're indicted, you're sent to prison. Three years later it comes out that one of the officers in your case was a liar."

—Joel Feinman, Pima County chief public defender

I was tipped off in May 2019 about a mistake that might affect hundreds of Pima County court defendants who had been found guilty or pleaded guilty to various crimes. An undetermined number of them were in jail or prison, according to the county's chief public defender.

It had to do with what's known as the "Brady List." That's the list of law enforcement employees found to have lied during their career (the name comes from a 1963 Supreme Court case). Their names must be turned over by prosecutors to the defense because their credibility could be questioned by a judge and jury, who would be aware that the law enforcement officer has a history of lying.

This story started with a fight in 2015 at a bar in Marana, Arizona, near Tucson. An off-duty Tucson police officer named Crystal Morales was found by TPD to have lied about her role in the altercation. Her brother-in-law had pulled a gun during the fight, and, according to police records, Morales first told Marana investigators she never saw the gun. She then told them she "heard a gun was drawn." She then told Tucson Police Department Internal Affairs investigators she had seen the gun.

A lieutenant recommended that Morales be fired, but she ended up getting suspended for a week. In early 2016, the Tucson Police Department sent a letter to the Pima county attorney's office about Morales's untruthfulness (prosecutors, which in most jurisdictions is the county attorney, are required to keep the Brady List current). I obtained a copy of TPD's letter. Pima county attorney Barbara LaWall should have immediately put Morales's name on the Brady List. She did not.

The county's chief public defender, Joel Feinman, told me, "Every citizen has the right to know if a witness who's going to be called against them is a liar or not. And the county attorney, it's their obligation to provide that."

I also obtained a letter that the chief criminal deputy in the county attorney's office sent in April 2019 to the public defender, acknowledging that Morales "should have been listed on the Brady List back in early 2016." According to Feinman, Officer Morales was involved in at least 200 cases during that two-and-a-half-year delay in her being placed on the list. Feinman said that meant that at least 200 people may have received tainted justice.

Feinman discussed the delayed listing in an interview. Speaking as if talking to a defendant, he said, "Is that a big deal to you that you didn't know about that the entire time? The prosecutor never told you, 'Hey, this officer who arrested you, this officer who interviewed witnesses, this officer our case depends on, is a liar. You went to prison without knowing that.' Is that a big deal? It's huge."

Jason Kreag, a law professor at the University of Arizona and a former criminal defense attorney, said, "This is a significant mistake. Here we have an officer who is known to have committed knowing falsehoods during an investigation of a very important crime, and this was evidence that could have impeached her credibility in every case that she was involved in. We need to know why she was left off the Brady List. Only the county attorney's office can answer that."

County Attorney LaWall declined my interview request, as she had done for all of my requests over the seven years that I worked in Tucson. LaWall rarely gave interviews. One of the few times I saw LaWall on camera was when she was confronted on the street in 2013 by *60 Minutes* reporter Steve Kroft. LaWall was seen walking away from Kroft while reluctantly answering a few questions. I thought it was a bad look and that any county's top attorney should be more cooperative with the media. Voters didn't seem bothered. LaWall was elected in 2016 to her sixth term in office.

My news director said to give LaWall a couple of days to respond to my interview request, and if she didn't, then I could approach her outside the building in which she worked. LaWall emailed me two days later. She said nothing about going on camera. She wrote, "We do not know exactly what happened that caused the omission" of Officer Morales from the Brady List. LaWall added that since 2015, Morales was involved in seventy-five cases. Feinman disagreed. "I'd say we have her in 200 cases," he said, again.

LaWall sent me a list of the closed cases in which Morales was involved. Almost all the defendants had pleaded guilty. Feinman said, "Those people who pled guilty might not have pled guilty if they had known that an officer involved in the case was on record as not telling the truth in an official investigation."

The letter from Tucson police to LaWall's office in 2016 about Officer Morales was sent to a woman who was then LaWall's chief criminal deputy. Her name is Kellie Johnson, and in 2019 she was a Pima County Superior Court judge. Johnson also declined an interview, saying through a court spokesperson that since she no longer worked for the county, "she does not want to assume, provide inaccurate information, try to recreate a situation, or comment on a letter that may or may not have been received by the County Attorney's office three years ago."

That sounded to me like Johnson was trying to deny any responsibility for the Brady List omission.

Professor Kreag said, "Someone clearly dropped the ball here. But ultimately it's the chief prosecutor's office, the elected prosecutor—here, Ms. LaWall's responsibility—to insure that her office complies with Brady. There's an investigation that needs to happen. The county attorney's office needs to figure out how this officer wasn't placed on the Brady List at the right time. It's their responsibility to do that."

I asked the chief public defender if he knew if this was an isolated mistake or if the county attorney had failed to inform defense attorneys about other cops who should be on Brady, possibly affecting the fate of more defendants. "That's really the important question right now," Feinman said. "And that's why it's so important to find out why this happened. Was this a systemic failure?"

There was another piece of information I thought should be included in the story. Feinman had run against LaWall in the 2016 Democratic primary and lost.

I told Feinman days after our interview that I needed to mention his primary loss on the air. He became angry and said in that case I could not do the story or air the interview. I pointed out how absurd that was, that the interview was the station's property. To his credit, Feinman relented. He's an attorney and knew he could not stop us from airing the interview. He realized it was my call whether to mention his loss to LaWall. I included it near the end of the piece. I did not want one person watching the piece to say, "That Feinman guy lost to LaWall and is just being sour grapes and Schwartz didn't mention that."

CHAPTER TWENTY-FOUR

Craigslist Con Man

SOUND BITE:

"He's a con man. But he's a sweet con man, ok? That's how he gets over. I'm sick to my stomach."

—Sarah Williams, ex live-in girlfriend of a guy she recently met,
after he vanished from her home because police were looking for him

I've done many stories about con artists who use Craigslist, the popular classified advertising website. Several viewers contacted me in the summer of 2013 about one such scammer.

They said Leonard Giso advertised two luxury apartments in Tucson for rent, but he wasn't the owner. I did a property search of tax assessor records and learned the apartments were owned by a man who I later discovered was one of Giso's friends. The friend gave Giso a key but not permission to sublet his apartment. The people who responded to the ads said Giso showed them the apartments while his friend was out of town. They said they paid Giso the first month's rent and a security deposit. He insisted on cash, a red flag they didn't pick up on. Then, they never saw Giso again, and he didn't answer their calls.

Before I set up interviews with the victims, I researched Giso. Prison records showed he had done time in Florida for grand theft. One of Giso's alleged victims, Curtis Galloway, told me Giso often bragged about being a heroic Army officer. "You know, he was the James Bond of the Army," Galloway said.

Based on Giso's prison record and the complaints about his apartment scam, I filed a public records request with the military. The records showed Giso served ten months, never rising above private, and was discharged after he went AWOL, twice.

The two-bedroom apartments that Giso listed were very nice, yet he was asking only $500 a month for them. Another red flag. I asked Galloway, "Did it occur to you that $500 rent for a luxury two-bedroom apartment was too low?" He said, "It did occur to me." Galloway thought he got lucky, that it was a great deal.

A man named Steve Fredricks said Giso also rented him an apartment. I had already obtained from Galloway the receipt that Giso had signed (in illegible handwriting). Before I interviewed Fredricks, I asked to see his receipt from Giso. It was dated April 6, 2013.

It was the same apartment Giso rented to Galloway hours later on the same day. Fredricks and Galloway had each given Giso hundreds of dollars.

And, as I liked to say on TV, there's more: Pima County sheriff's deputies said Giso was wanted on five charges, including four felonies—two for fraud, two for forgery, and one misdemeanor for theft of services. Those charges were for a different case. Investigators said Giso went on dates with women he met online, used Town cars and never paid the company. The owner of the transportation company, 520 Express, told me that Giso provided paperwork showing he was with a business and had set up a corporate account. The car service didn't require upfront payment with its corporate accounts. Giso used the service's cars for almost a month, then disappeared. The owner of 520 Express said he had researched the corporate account, but realized later that Giso had transposed the account's last two numbers.

One of the women that the fifty-one-year-old Giso took on a date in a Town car he never paid for was roughly half his age. Sarah Williams said she met Giso on Ok Cupid, the online dating site. She let him live with her for about six weeks. Sarah told me Giso found out that detectives were looking for him. One day while she was out, Giso left. She never saw him again. I asked her, "If you could talk to Giso now, what would you say?" Sarah replied, "You reap what you sow."

A sheriff's department detective told me, "There's an active warrant for his arrest. He's moving, so people can't find him." Investigators received a tip that Giso might be in the Atlanta area, where he lived before moving to Tucson.

Giso was arrested near Atlanta about three months after our initial story on him aired. Sources told me that someone in the Peach State had seen our story online. That someone didn't think Giso was a peach; she claimed he ripped her off, too, and she called the cops.

Giso was extradited to Tucson and before his trial turned down a plea deal that would have given him a maximum sentence of twelve and a half years. He gave me a dirty look when he entered the courtroom.

It took the jury barely an hour to find Giso guilty of four felonies, two each for fraud (for the apartment rental scam) and forgery (for the false information on the car service paperwork). He showed no emotion when the judge sentenced him to eighteen and a half years in prison. By declining the plea deal and taking his chance with a jury trial, he added six years to his sentence.

The first victim of Giso's apartment scam was Steve Fredericks. Outside the courthouse after the sentencing, Fredericks said, "He doesn't really have a conscience, between right or wrong. He just has that pattern of burning people all his adult life."

Months later I received a letter from an inmate at a state prison in Tucson. It was one of hundreds of letters inmates have sent to me proclaiming their innocence. At the end of the inmate's letter, the guy wrote, "P.S. My cellmate says hello. His name is Leonard Giso."

CHAPTER TWENTY-FIVE

You Can Run but You Can't Hide

SOUND BITE:

"There is no line that she won't cross, and no end to the level of her deception."

—Joe Murphy, on his ex-girlfriend, Rebecca Burke

Rebecca burke was five-feet, six-inches tall and weighed 225 pounds. She was thirty-three years old and had already done three prison stints for fraud and theft. Burke's preteen daughter lived with relatives while she did jail time, according to sources. Those are not things you'd put in an online dating profile, unless it was on "Meet-an-inmate.com." Yet Burke had no trouble attracting men. One of them was a Tucson resident named Joe Murphy.

Joe contacted me in 2015 a year after he met Burke on the dating site Plenty of Fish, he said. She eventually moved in with him and he gave her his life savings— $19,000, Murphy told me.

Burke claimed she had cancer, and showed Joe a doctor's letter attesting to that. She typed the letter herself using a clinic's letterhead. She said she was also in tough shape financially, but was a trust fund baby and would soon be receiving seven million dollars. Murphy and another of Burke's boyfriends told me she claimed that her father was a wealthy property owner but disappeared, was captured by a Mexican cartel and killed. She claimed her mother was a Pima County Superior Court judge. I found out that judge does not have a daughter.

Joe made the same mistake I've seen in countless stories: someone falls fast for someone they met recently or feels sorry for them or both. He also fell for Burke's fantastic stories. "She was just so convincing," he said. "And she showed me the doctor's letter about her cancer, and I felt sorry for her."

Joe was new to Tucson and was lonely. He rented a nice house and had a good job. He also admitted he was excited about Burke soon having access to a trust fund. But he said he legitimately liked her. For a while.

After I discovered Burke's prison record, I felt I had a story. People can turn their lives around. But based on the stories Burke told Joe, it appeared she hadn't changed.

Joe told me that Burke lived with him for about a year and drained his savings by buying clothes and dining out often. After several months, Joe told her to get a job. Joe was pleased when Burke told him she landed a position as a secretary at a car dealership. Since she didn't have a car, Joe dropped her off at the bus stop every weekday and picked her up there ten hours later.

Joe said a month after Burke told him she was working, she hadn't given him a penny towards his bills. His savings account was down to nothing. Burke told me that on Christmas Day 2015, he demanded to see one of her pay stubs. Joe said Burke broke down and told Joe the truth—she had no job.

I asked Joe the obvious question: "You dropped her off at the bus stop every morning and picked her up at night. Did you ask her what she was doing during those ten hours in between?"

He said, "No. I was past that and wouldn't believe anything she said anyway."

Joe kicked Burke out of his house. Joe said he discovered later that the two valuable guns he kept in the attic were stolen by Burke. He filed a police report. Burke disappeared.

About a month after my story aired, I received a phone call from a woman in San Diego. She worked as a groomer in a pet store in nearby Escondido and said a woman named Rebecca Burke started working there two days earlier. The tipster said during Burke's second day on the job, some employees had items stolen from their purses. There was no proof Burke did it (she was never charged), but the caller said she had a bad feeling about Burke, so she Googled her. Our story popped up and the tipster realized her new colleague was the same person under investigation by the Pima County Sheriff's Department for stealing from Joe Murphy.

I asked the tipster about Burke's work schedule. She said that every morning at around 10:30, Burke went on a break and smoked cigarettes near her car. Burke had somehow acquired money to get a vehicle. The tipster said it was a gray Mazda.

I told my news director that a photographer and I needed to go to Escondido, and she agreed. Two days later, we sat outside the pet store in our unmarked news van. Right around 10:30 a.m., a short, heavyset woman with glasses came outside. She walked over to a gray Mazda, opened the door, took out a pack of cigarettes and lit up.

We got out of the news van and approached her with the camera rolling.

"Hi, Rebecca. I'm Matthew Schwartz with the News 4 Tucson Investigators," I said in my usual cordial way. She started taking quick drags on her cigarette while walking from her car to the store, about 100 feet away. She wanted to get inside, where we couldn't go. All of the pet store's employees were watching by now, those on break outside, and those inside. It's not every day a news crew shows up to confront an employee.

I walked alongside Burke and peppered her with a half dozen questions about the allegations. She said nothing. Finally, nearing the store's entrance, she said something that seemed funny and ironic, considering her felony record and the current accusations against her. She said, "You're not supposed to be here." While Burke said that, she flicked her cigarette away, close to my face. The shot ended up in a promo for our investigative unit that ran for months.

This follow-up report aired a few days later. I started it by paraphrasing the classic line from boxing icon Joe Louis: "Rebecca Burke could run, but she couldn't hide."

The next day I spoke with a Tucson Police Department investigator who was very interested in getting the specifics on Burke's whereabouts.

I then received a tip from a Tucson police detective. Burke apparently fled again. Seemed she was fired from the pet store after the company also Googled her following our confrontation. Kind of late for a background check. This time Burke went from San Diego to Alaska.

A few weeks later I received a tip from law enforcement that Burke had been arrested in Anchorage. She was living with Ken Wilson, who owned a business there and told me he too met Burke on Plenty of Fish. Ken claimed Burke told him the same lies she had allegedly told Joe Murphy, but with a new twist. She told the man she was a nanny for a wealthy San Diego couple. "She said the couple was going to move, buy her a house and give her a million dollars to help her because they felt bad for her," Ken said.

Ken couldn't believe how gullible he was. He paid for her airfare from California to Alaska. I interviewed Wilson via FaceTime from our Tucson studio. He said Alaska state troopers showed up at his house one day and sat in a car out front, unbeknownst to him. When he came outside to get into his truck to drive to work, investigators approached. They showed him photos of Burke, along with thirty-six aliases she had used. Ken said she told him her name was Rebecca Elise. The investigators asked Wilson if he knew where Burke was now. "Yeah," he said. "She's inside my house." They went inside and arrested Burke without incident, but with another ironic line from her. According to Ken, as she was being escorted out in handcuffs, Burke turned to Ken and said, "I'll call you from jail." She did call, and Ken didn't answer.

Burke was extradited to Tucson. She pleaded guilty to trafficking in stolen property for stealing Joe Murphy's guns. She wasn't charged in Alaska because Ken Wilson willingly gave her money. Murphy, now broke, wanted Burke to get the maximum of eight years in prison. He was in the courtroom for sentencing, and we were, too.

Burke was represented by a public defender. She couldn't afford a private attorney. I remember thinking, *I guess Burke still hasn't received the millions from her two trust funds.* I also thought it would add something to the story if the sentencing judge was the same one who Burke claimed to be her mother. Would Burke say "Yes, your honor" or "Yes, Mom?" Reporters spend a lot of downtime in courtrooms, and I often thought of humorous things to entertain myself. But it was a different judge. And no laughing matter for Joe Murphy.

Burke's lawyer said Burke's childhood was "tragic" and said she was "bounced around foster homes" and that "she's sorry about what happened in this case."

Burke was stoic when she entered the courtroom but started crying after the judge sentenced her to three and a half years in prison.

Outside the courthouse, Joe said, "I'm not happy with the sentence. I do take solace in the fact that she will be behind bars for three and a half years."

I nagged the prosecutor in the Burke case, Kellie Johnson, for an interview and she reluctantly agreed.

"Mr. Murphy, the victim, wanted eight years and she got three and a half. Additionally, Burke had three prior convictions. What do you think of the sentence?"

Johnson said, "Well, the judge has to weigh all of the facts and circumstances in the case and here found that the presumptive, or middle sentence, was appropriate based on the aggravation and mitigation in front of her."

A boring, legalese sound bite, but the best I could get.

Burke was sent to the county jail where she'd be held until being transferred to a state prison. I called the jail a few days later and requested an interview with her. She agreed. I was a little surprised, but not shocked. I think she was narcissistic and enjoyed the attention.

Arizona doesn't permit on-camera interviews in its state prisons. That's always bothered me. In New York I was allowed to interview a serial killer in a maximum-security prison, but in Arizona, inmate interviews have to be done on the phone. Phone interviews are great for radio but a last resort on TV, except during breaking news, such as when you need to hear from an eyewitness or first responder.

On the morning of the interview in county jail with Burke, a photographer and I arrived early and waited in a captain's office. A female officer said she would tell Burke and the corrections officers that we were there. The officer returned about ten minutes later and gave us bad news. Burke was gone. She had been transferred a couple of hours earlier to a state prison. I learned something that day. I should have requested the interview immediately following her sentencing, as soon as she was in the county jail.

Three years later, in February 2019, I received a call in the newsroom. It was Rebecca Burke. She had recently been released and wanted to do an interview. She said she was living in the Phoenix area and had a good job. I asked her what she would say on camera, and she claimed she'd come clean on stealing her ex-boyfriend's guns but did nothing else wrong. She said she would deny lying to Ken Wilson. I didn't ask her why she used thirty-six aliases.

Her story was, by then, old news with nothing substantively different other than her release from jail. I wished her the best and politely declined her offer to do an interview.

CHAPTER TWENTY-SIX

Food Bank Failure

SOUND BITE:

"He made himself out to be this savior, that he was doing God's work. And he turned himself into the Devil."

—Tammi Coles, a food bank donor, after learning that the charity's CEO allegedly took money that was supposed to buy food for the needy

Some viewers told me in October 2013 that a man who ran a food bank near Tucson was using its funds as his personal piggy bank.

I met with several angry members of the board of directors and donors for the Vail Community Food Bank. The nonprofit gave food to more than 300 people every two weeks. The food bank had to close recently due to financial problems.

A board member handed me the charity's checking account statements for three months. The only person with access to the account, through a food bank debit card, was its CEO and director, Anthony Bustamante.

143

Bustamante was only supposed to buy items needed for the food bank's central drop-off building and adjacent office. Light bulbs and those sorts of things. But the bank statements showed the thirty-eight-year-old Vail resident bought personal items. Transactions he charged to the food bank included "Colorado River Adventures" for $627; "T-Mobile" for $249; "Vail Vikings Youth Football" for $100. There were many other charges and ATM withdrawals.

Internal Revenue Service regulations state, "No part of a 501 (c) 3 organization may benefit a private shareholder or individual."

Again, some stories are layups, some you work hard to prove. This was a layup. It was rare that a tipster provided all the proof I needed.

I interviewed a half dozen board members and donors. Board member Tiffany Harris said, "Anthony is a snake in the grass. I'm sorry I have to say it like that, but that's how I feel." Sandy Skaja and her husband, Tim, had recently donated $600 to the food bank. Sandy said when she learned of the transactions, "I just kind of felt violated; I felt like I'd been cheated. There are people who rely on the food bank and are hurting. It's just inexcusable."

A food bank volunteer named David Hessel quit a few months earlier when he became disillusioned. Hessel said that Bustamante had him load the charity's truck with donated items and found out later that Bustamante brought them to his house.

It was time for me to find Mr. Bustamante. He had some explaining to do.

I didn't think if I called Bustamante that he would do an interview after I told him I had the bank statements. So, a photographer and I sat in our news van outside his house. After a few hours, his garage door opened, and he drove off. We followed him for about twenty minutes on I-10, a busy highway. He was driving about ninety miles per hour, but my photographer, who was driving, didn't lose him. I was not relaxed.

Bustamante pulled off the highway and parked near a complex of baseball and softball fields. His young daughter was apparently playing there.

I didn't want to make a scene in front of the kids or parents or embarrass Bustamante's daughter. But I had to interview him. Fortunately, Bustamante stopped walking far from the closest field. No one was near us. He didn't see us until we were a few feet away. He seemed surprised.

I asked Bustamante, "Did you ever make any ATM withdrawals with the Vail Community Food Bank debit card for your own personal expenses?"

"No, I did not," he said. "I used it all for the Vail Community Food Bank."

Only then did I show him the bank statements. His answers changed. We had this exchange:

Me: "Where did this money come from that you used to purchase the river adventure trip, textbooks, numerous Starbucks, Circle Ks, and ATM withdrawals on the food bank's debit card?"

Bustamante: "Okay, I'll explain it to you. All the money that came from me, I sold the stuff from my house 'cause I'm moving. So, what I did was, I used this 'cause I didn't have another card, another credit card or anything, so I used this to make the transactions because these people don't take cash."

I knew those merchants did indeed accept cash.

Bustamante went on to explain that he used the food bank's debit card because he didn't have a personal checking account. He claimed he deposited money to make up for his withdrawals and purchases. The statements showed he did make some deposits, but they fell hundreds of dollars short of what he spent.

Me: "You did admit to me, did you not, that you used the food bank's debit card?"

Bustamante: "I have to go. My daughter's here now. I appreciate your time. Thank you very much."

How polite!

His daughter's game ended and she was approaching us. I told the photographer we had enough. We stopped shooting and returned to our car.

But there was more. Board members said before the food bank closed, Bustamante told them he would take the hundreds of cans of food out of its office and distribute them to a nearby food bank, the Greater Vail Community Services.

I went to that nonprofit and interviewed its director, Mark Tate. "We never received any of the food," Tate said. I told Tate that Bustamante had promised to give him the food. "Right," Tate said, "but sometimes Mr. Bustamante would say one thing and do another."

I think many news organizations don't do enough follow-up stories. I've been asked countless times by viewers, "Whatever happened with that guy (or woman)?" And "How'd that story end up?" I decided to revisit this one several months later. A spokesperson with the Pima County Sheriff's Department told me, "We are actively investigating the possible fraudulent use of their funds."

People who knew Bustamante said he split town soon after our first report aired. As of early 2020, his whereabouts were unknown and he had not been charged in the case.

CHAPTER TWENTY-SEVEN

Irrigation Irritation

SOUND BITE:

"I'm just absolutely heartbroken. We live on a fixed income and we saved for this."

—Tucson resident Kathy Brothers after she and her husband lost
thousands to an unlicensed home contractor

The dozens of reports I did on unlicensed home contractors had common threads and, usually, sad endings. Homeowners who did little research before hiring a home repairman or installer would often hire someone just because he had the lowest bid. Sometimes they hired based on one recommendation from a friend or neighbor. Unscrupulous contractors would do little or no work after getting the first payment, then disappear.

Kathy Brothers called me in 2018 with her contractor nightmare. She and her husband needed a new backyard irrigation system at their home. Kathy did a little research before hiring a company called Desert Drip Irrigation. She said she saw a few positive reviews for the company on Google. I explained to her how some companies

147

post fake reviews from family members and friends. Kathy never called the Arizona Registrar of Contractors or checked its website. If she had, she would have known that "Desert Drip Irrigation" was not licensed in Arizona. The state requires a contractor's license for jobs of $1,000 or more.

Kathy is a retired military nurse, and she and her husband were living on fixed incomes. She told me the company's owner twice delayed the start of the job and made up various excuses when he didn't show, including a rainy forecast. He insisted he'd be at her house on the third day he was scheduled to start.

"He never showed," Kathy said. "So, I called, I texted him. And nothing. Absolutely nothing. And to this day, there's been no call, no response to any of my emails or phone calls."

When I called the company, its owner, Gustavo Ruiz, was friendly when he answered the phone. Maybe he thought a potential customer was calling. Then I told him I was investigating Kathy's complaints.

Ruiz hung up on me. Minutes later, the company's website was taken down. Fortunately, I already had a screenshot of it saved for use in our story.

I always took screenshots of people and businesses I was investigating before I called them, knowing they might quickly remove all online information and photos. One night, my story on another scam artist aired. He was a satellite TV installer. While he was at customers' homes, especially those of elderly women, he convinced them they needed a new TV. He took their money and never returned, much less delivered a TV. I found photos of him on his wife's Facebook page. I saved them for the story. Less than five minutes after the piece aired, complete with photos of him, I checked his wife's Facebook. His photos were deleted. Too late. He was later indicted for fraud and theft of services.

The website for the irrigation company whose owner, Ruiz, vanished on Kathy didn't include his photo. I wanted viewers to know what Ruiz looked like in case he pitched business to them—

and in case he changed the name of his business. Crooked businesses often change names but usually not their crooked ways. Before the company's website was removed, I jotted down its address. A photographer and I went there. It was a UPS store. Ruiz might have had a box there, but his business apparently did not have a physical location. Another bad sign.

When I arrived at work the day after the irrigation scam story aired, I had several messages from contractors. They offered to install a free irrigation system in Kathy's yard. Kathy and her husband happily accepted.

I felt good for this hardworking, retired couple. Also, I would have another story. I always needed more stories. It's what's known in the business as "feeding the beast." It means providing content for the newscasts and website. And the impactful results of a story are called "proof of performance." It showed viewers that we got results.

CHAPTER TWENTY-EIGHT

Travel Trouble

SOUND BITE:

"It's clear-cut. This was a campaign trip and he did it on taxpayer time."

—Tom Ryan, attorney and political watchdog,
on Arizona House Speaker David Gowan

D avid Gowan was the arizona Speaker of the House but looked more cowboy than politician. The conservative Republican from Sierra Vista was rarely seen without a ten-gallon hat and cowboy boots. His boots figuratively stepped in doo-doo during his 2016 campaign for Congress.

After announcing his candidacy for a seat in Congressional District 1, Gowan was driven, in a state-owned vehicle, to numerous events around the massive district—bigger than the state of Illinois. The car was marked "For Official Use Only." Gowan also reportedly used a state employee as his driver—Sergeant at Arms Billy Cloud for the Arizona State House, whose annual salary was $80,000. Pretty expensive driver, paid with taxpayers dollars.

Arizona law prohibits state employees from using state vehicles

150

for personal use. The law also says state resources cannot be used to "influence an election."

Gowan tweeted several photos while traveling the state. On October 8, the caption under a photo from Flagstaff read, "Listening to voters & talking about my vision to make DC accountable." During a radio interview that same day, he said, "What do we need in Washington, DC? Nineteen trillion in the hole? We need somebody who's capable of bringing those ideas and fighting for those issues down there."

I saw this story in the *Arizona Capitol Times*. It was a solid piece of investigative reporting but did not have an interview with Gowan. He declined comment through his spokesperson, Stephanie Grisham. I thought I could advance the story by finding Gowan and asking him about using a state car for what certainly appeared to be campaigning for Congress.

A photographer and I went to the statehouse in Phoenix to get video of Gowan on the House floor. We were upstairs in the public gallery when a security guard tried to kick us out. This was the area where anyone could watch elected officials in session, and there was a sizable audience. I was incredulous about being told to leave, and I refused. I told the photographer to record the attempted ejection. The guard returned a few minutes later and said we could stay.

Gowan declined an interview through the spokesperson for the Republican representatives. I needed to question him face-to-face or I'd have the same story the *Capitol Times* had. Surprisingly, when I looked online for Gowan's schedule of campaign events I found none. I called several sources and one told me that Gowan had a "meet and greet" with potential voters that Saturday at a restaurant in a Tucson suburb.

The photographer and I were outside the restaurant when Gowan arrived. An aide asked us what we needed. I told him I wanted to ask Gowan about his campaign. That was true. I did not tell the aide or need to tell him my specific questions. If I had, I don't think I would have gotten the interview. The aide said, "Sure, I'll bring him over to you after the meet and greet."

After lobbing some softball questions about how his campaign was going, I asked, "What about that October 8 radio interview in Flagstaff, where you *did* talk about going to Washington, DC, with a state vehicle taking you to that interview?" He replied, "Right. So the point here is you're not going to separate the Speaker from the candidate. And they asked me about it. What am I going to do, decline?"

That's exactly what he should have done, according to state law.

State Representative Bruce Wheeler, a Democrat from Tucson and then a member of the House Ethics Committee, had this reaction: "I think this does not pass any smell test." Wheeler pointed out that Gowan was regularly provided a driver from the Arizona Department of Public Safety, but said DPS wanted no part of this trip. "One can only speculate that the DPS driver was not going to drive him around to campaign events," Wheeler said. Sources told me that Gowan then asked a buddy, the aforementioned Sergeant at Arms Billy Cloud, to be his driver.

I asked Gowan, "Why didn't you take your DPS driver on that trip instead of Billy Cloud?" He said, "You know, who knows why? I go out there and take these vehicles and travel around. I have a . . . he's my sergeant at arms, so he was taking me to certain different areas. It's just the same and sometimes those drivers aren't regularly ready."

At the end of our interview, Gowan revealed that he had reimbursed the state for the trip. That raised this obvious question, as I said in the piece: "If, as Speaker Gowan and his staff claim, he did nothing wrong, then why was the state reimbursed?"

We requested documentation from the Department of Administration. Records showed that four days after the *Capitol Times* broke the story, Gowan paid the state back more than $12,000 for mileage and per diem reimbursements.

The spokesperson, Grisham, said in an email that the reimbursement was due to a "staff miscommunication." She said Gowan ordered a review of records related to his use of fleet vehicles for 2015 and it found "every fleet rental was supported by valid state business travel." But Grisham added the review "also revealed situations in which the Speaker was improperly reimbursed for mileage. There were many instances where the Speaker's assistant assumed incorrectly that he was driving his personal vehicle when in fact he was using a fleet vehicle. When the discrepancy came to light, the Speaker immediately made full repayment by personal check."

I was supposed to believe that Gowan's assistant never asked him which car he took. It sounded to me as though either Gowan or Grisham, maybe both, threw the assistant under the bus. Or in this case, under a state-owned car. It was political public relations 101: It's never the politician's fault. Blame an unknown, low-level staffer.

Grisham said the reimbursement included more than $1,600 for some days Gowan claimed to work but didn't.

Tom Ryan, an attorney and political watchdog from Chandler, said the attorney general needed do the investigation instead of Gowan's staff. Ryan said, "Ha. Them investigating themselves is a joke. That's like a bank robber being asked to investigate his own bank robbery. They're going to find, 'Hey, no bank robbery here.'"

I received an angry email from Grisham on the Monday following my interview with him. She was upset that I approached Gowan after she told me he declined to be interviewed.

Not long after the story ran, polls showed Gowan near the bottom of a large pack of candidates running for the congressional seat. He dropped out of the race.

Grisham fared better. After working for Donald Trump's 2016 presidential campaign, she became Melania Trump's press secretary. She later was named Trump's press secretary.

CHAPTER TWENTY-NINE

Kiosk Chaos

SOUND BITE:

"We need more investigative reporting in Tucson. There are a lot of scam artists there."

—A long-time Tucson resident

On my flight from Tampa to Tucson in April 2013 to start working at KVOA, a doctor and his wife were sitting next to me. They had lived in Tucson for years, and I had never been there prior to my job interview two months earlier. The doctor told me, "There are a lot of scams there you need to investigate." I thought, *Bad for the honest, hardworking residents, but good for an investigate reporter.* I would soon learn the doctor's concerns were well placed. As you have read by now, Tucson produced a plethora of stories involving scam artists.

One story came in my first year in town from two young women who said their new jobs turned out to be a con job. They were sisters named Claudia Acevo and Racquel Montanez. They had worked for two weeks selling cell phone protectors for a company called Invisible Shield. The franchise had a kiosk at a local mall. They claimed they were never paid and that the woman who identified herself as the franchise's owner owed them almost $1,800 each. The sisters said they couldn't afford to pay their rent without the money.

This investigation became very interesting and had an unusual ending.

Raquel said the franchise owner, Tammy Cannito, recruited them with talk of bright futures and good money. "She told us we'd make about two thousand dollars bi-weekly, plus 42 percent commission," Racquel said. I thought, *42 percent, really?* The women claimed Cannito also told them she would pay for their health insurance. The sisters were so excited they quit longtime jobs to work at the kiosk.

Claudia said, "After just a few days, the owner was telling us we could move up in the company. It sounded too good to be true. Everybody told me that."

As usual when something sounds too good to be true, it was.

After working at the kiosk for a week, the sisters became suspicious. They hadn't been given any hiring-related paperwork and couldn't log on to the company's payroll site. They said the owner blamed everything on a technical glitch. Claudia said Cannito told her, "I promise you, I promise you, there won't be a problem" in them getting paid.

Their first paychecks, due on May 5, 2014, didn't come. Although they had no timesheets showing their hours, they showed me text messages from Cannito saying they'd be paid the next day, blaming the delay on another technical problem. On May 6, Claudia texted Cannito, "So when will I have my check?" The reply: "By 3 at the latest."

Later that day, Cannito sent another text (the sisters saved the texts and we showed them in the report). She said she was about to deposit the women's combined paycheck of nearly $3,600 into Raquel's account. I thought, *What kind of business pays two employees with one check?* But the women believed it. "I'll call you when it's all done," Cannito texted them.

The sisters were still waiting to be paid when they contacted me three weeks later.

It was time to ask Tammy Cannito some questions. I knew what she looked like from her photos on social media. We found her sitting on a bench outside the mall, smoking a cigarette. We walked up to her with the camera rolling.

After I introduced myself in my standard friendly way, I asked Cannito for her job title. "I'm a sales rep," she said. She claimed she never told the women she was the owner. Then she said the women never worked at the kiosk.

"They didn't work here?" I asked.

"No," she said.

I told her, "I've seen the texts you sent them promising you'd pay them. Why did you send those texts if they didn't work here?"

She answered, "I have no idea, I don't know. I'm not even going to go into this right now."

I replied, "Well, I'm trying to get your side of the story." She got up and walked back into the mall. I followed her and asked, "Why are you walking away?" No answer.

Racquel had told me she drove Cannito to work some days. The sisters said they and Cannito always worked the same shifts, with no other employees. There was a reason.

Tammy Cannito was *not* the franchise's owner. She was, the company later found, getting paid for the hours the sisters worked, receiving three salaries.

I returned to the newsroom, and once I saw that the interview came out fine, I called the corporate office for Invisible Shield and provided all the details. I purposely hadn't called sooner because I didn't want Cannito to know we were onto her and possibly split town or quit the job before I could confront her. I thought viewers needed to see her face.

Cannito got fired by the kiosk's real owner, a woman named Jordan Scott. After I told Scott the story, she confirmed the details with the victims.

Scott met the sisters later that week and gave them their paychecks. We were there recording. Scott said, "Today I want to present each of you with a check for the full amount of the hours, and thank you so much for coming forward."

Claudia said, "Now we don't have to worry about not being able to pay our bills. We're both grateful for News 4 Tucson. And for Jordan as well to do what she did, because she didn't have to."

The three women hugged, and Jordan told them, "I'm really sorry that this happened."

The sisters wanted to move past this and said they would apply for jobs at the same kiosk. Real jobs. Jordan said she'd make sure all the required paperwork would be filled out.

CHAPTER THIRTY

Lost in Translation

SOUND BITE:

"I hate it. I think it's like telling a racist joke."

—Clarence Boykins, an African American community activist,
on certain pictures shown in class by a high school teacher

A story I did in 2015 was unlike any I had done before. When you've done thousands of stories, they begin to repeat in slightly different forms. Besides this one being original, I thought it would interest viewers and create some buzz.

The mother of a senior at Vail High School near Tucson called me and was furious about something her son's Spanish teacher did in class. Cecelia Hailey and her son, Nazareth, said the teacher showed students photos of celebrities and asked them to use Spanish words to identify the emotions the photos depicted. The problem was, the photos were doctored, and in a bad way. President Obama was shown with big lips and huge ears; Oprah Winfrey had numerous neck rolls. Not all the photos were of black people. Jennifer Aniston's nose looked like Pinocchio's.

Nazareth, who is African American, said the teacher also made inappropriate comments. When a picture of Ronald McDonald was shown, Nazareth claimed the teacher said, "I don't know if Ronald McDonald is a boy or a girl because I don't know what's down there in his pants." Simply a bizarre comment.

I began the piece by saying, "If a picture tells a thousand words, what words would you use to describe this picture of President Obama?"

Regarding the caricatures of Obama and Winfrey, Nazareth said, "I was disgusted, embarrassed. I felt degraded as an African American. I felt kind of humiliated."

When Winfrey's photo was shown with the doctored neck rolls, the teacher said Winfrey looked "terrible," using the Spanish word for terrible. Nazareth, the only African American in the class, said when the teacher showed Obama's photo, "Everyone in the class burst out laughing. I honestly wanted to get up and walk out and not come back. But I had to sit there because my grades are important to me."

I interviewed Vail Schools superintendent Calvin Baker. He said he found out about the photos only after Nazareth's mother complained to the teacher. Baker and I had this exchange:

Baker: "As soon as she found out that it was offensive to someone, she pulled those pictures."

Me: "But should she have to be told that it's offensive? Shouldn't a teacher of young people know that that's [the Obama caricature] an offensive picture without being told?"

Baker: "You know, it was an error in judgment, and we all make errors in judgment from time to time."

I thought if this happened in New York, Los Angeles, Philadelphia, or any other city with large African American populations, it would prompt strong reactions. I could see protests and calls for the teacher to be suspended or fired. Can you imagine the outcries from social media and the cable television networks if they saw this story? The reaction in Tucson, which has an African American population of under 5 percent, was apathetic. I received only about a dozen calls and emails from viewers who were outraged by the teacher's actions. I didn't want the teacher to get fired. I thought she needed some training on race, sensitivity, and just common sense.

Mrs. Hailey agreed, saying, "I by no means want her fired. I think she does need some severe counseling and maybe some redirection and some more teacher education."

I had been working with the school district's media relations director who was, as you'd expect, upset that I was reporting this. Promos for the piece aired for about twenty-four hours beforehand. The morning the story was to air on our 10 p.m. newscast, the media director showed up in the TV station lobby. I wasn't there but was told she was in tears. I was told she tried to persuade my news director to kill the piece. To my boss's credit, she refused.

The teacher was in her tenth year at the high school and headed its foreign language department. She was named Teacher of the Year multiple times, which I reported. She declined an interview but apologized in a statement, saying, "I was made aware that the parent of one of my students was offended by some of the images used. I immediately contacted the parent to apologize and shared that I would be changing the slideshow for future use. . . . I am deeply sorry for offending anyone with the images that I selected and want all of my students and parents to know that I have their best interest at heart."

Superintendent Baker said about the Obama picture, "We apologize for using that picture. We take responsibility for it. It won't be used again. . . . Changes are being made, improvements are being made."

Local African American business leader Clarence Boykins said, "To say 'I'm sorry,' what does that mean? We need to know why [the teacher did this]." The Tucson Urban League issued a statement about the picture of President Obama: "This photo reinforces negative racist stereotypes and is disrespectful to not only the president, but to African Americans. It is unfortunate that this teacher, who is responsible for molding young minds, would choose to use this photo in a classroom setting."

I couldn't have agreed more. I thought if the class was about racism and the teacher was illustrating examples of it, maybe the pictures could be shown in that vein. Because some of the pictures sure were racist. But to show them as a way of teaching Spanish words? Why not just show undoctored photos of Obama, Winfrey, and the others and ask students how they would describe those?

Most of the reactions I received from viewers were positive. A few thought I was too tough on the teacher. I disagreed. Although the story didn't create a big buzz, it did win the year's regional Edward R. Murrow Award for Investigative Reporting. I hope it was seen by a lot of teachers, especially any who needed sensitivity training.

CHAPTER THIRTY-ONE

Amazon Anxiety

SOUND BITE:

"Schwartz is gonna ruin the whole deal."

—A millionaire Tucson businessman, after I reported specific plans about an
Amazon warehouse to be built in the city

Many civic and business leaders don't understand that reporters are not supposed to be cheerleaders. As citizens, it's great if the town we live in is prosperous. As journalists, we are supposed to report the good, the bad, and the ugly.

A story I reported in March 2018 is a good example of this misunderstanding. A trade magazine called *Arizona Builder's Exchange* broke a story about online retail giant Amazon building a large warehouse in Tucson. It would bring 1,500 to 2,000 much-needed jobs. It would be a big boost for the city's image as well as its economy.

I wanted to see if I could confirm the magazine's details and advance the story. I made a few calls, and a city official soon sent me very specific details about what insiders had code-named "Project Wildcat," after the University of Arizona's mascot.

162

My source sent me the official draft of the project's plans, complete with all the engineering companies' names, the exact location of the warehouse, and the square footage. I reported all this and credited the magazine for breaking the story. I also reported that we wanted to speak with Pima County officials about the project, but everyone declined. I was struck by how strongly and quickly they declined. You would have thought this was a matter of national security, which, by the way, I would not report if it meant possibly endangering anyone.

I found out that nondisclosure agreements had been signed by the principals. I emailed the county administrator, Chuck Huckelberry, who replied, "No one will talk about it."

A note about Huckelberry: I did a story on his annual salary of $320,000, which made him the highest-paid county administrator in Arizona and among the top in the country. Yet afterwards he cooperated with me and never declined an interview request. More thin-skinned officials would ignore a reporter after a story like that. I told him I appreciated his understanding. He said the story was accurate and he had no hard feelings. Hey, it's not his fault the board of supervisors voted to pay him that much; I wouldn't turn it down.

For the Amazon story, I contacted Sun Corridor, a group that works on bringing jobs and investment growth to the region. Its spokesperson emailed me a statement: "Due to non-disclosure agreements and board policy on confidentiality, we are not able to share project information."

I called the project engineers, the development's property company, and the architect; no one returned my calls. I filed a public records request with the county, asking for any documents mentioning Amazon, Project Wildcat, or Century Park (the name of the business complex where the warehouse was going to be built). The response: "Pima County has entered into a Non-Disclosure Agreement with the developer of these properties and are (sic) in the process of notifying the company of the public records request.

The company has 10 days from the date of notification to provide a court order protecting the information per the NDA."

County officials would not even confirm that the company was Amazon, and Amazon wouldn't comment.

The director of the Goldwater Institute, a conservative think tank based in Phoenix, said he thought the nondisclosure agreements violated Arizona's public records law. Jon Riches told me, "You can't keep secret the public's business, and the company, in this case Amazon, should very well know that, if they're seeking to enter into business with a government entity."

I reported this on March 28, 2018. The next morning my news director called me. She said she had just received a call from a well-known local businessman. He owned a multimillion-dollar company. My boss said the guy was furious about my story, that it could cause Amazon to cancel its deal. I thought that was crazy and maybe he was more concerned about losing potential business if the deal fell through. I hardly thought Amazon's bean counters would cancel a potentially lucrative deal, all because of a local news report.

The millionaire's concerns weren't necessary. A few months later, Amazon announced plans to build the warehouse in, yes, Tucson.

CHAPTER THIRTY-TWO

Police Chief Pouts

SOUND BITE:

"These people will be the least armed people in the park."

—A homeless man on the Tucson Police Department using unarmed community service officers to patrol city parks

T ucson's police chief, Chris Magnus, was named to the job in January 2016 and through early 2020 declined all three or four of my interview requests. I never even talked to the guy on the phone.

I was never told why he refused to speak with me or be interviewed. My guess is that I was *persona non grata* because of a story I did in 2018 called "Deadly Delay." The piece was about police taking more than four hours to respond to a 911 call.

On May 6, 2018, a woman named April Barbosa was worried that her daughter was in danger. Her worry was warranted. Eighteen-year-old Rosaura Hernandez had broken up with her live-in boyfriend the night before and went back to his apartment to retrieve her things. Rosaura arrived at 10 a.m. Her family first called 911 at around 1 p.m.

165

after Rosaura did not reply to their texts or calls. She usually replied immediately.

The police showed up at 5:30 p.m. and didn't break down the door when no one answered. They said they couldn't do so because the lease was in the boyfriend's name. The leasing office was closed, so cops couldn't get a key. Officers left the scene. At 7 p.m., the family, now frantic, returned to the apartment. A family member broke a window and entered the apartment. Rosaura's battered body was on the kitchen floor. The medical examiner said she was stabbed multiple times and strangled. The ex-boyfriend was charged with her murder. He pleaded guilty in February 2020.

The family's attorney said Rosaura might be alive if officers had responded four hours earlier and broken into the apartment. He announced a lawsuit against the police department and the city.

I requested an interview with TPD a week before the story ran. I received no response or even an email statement until 2:20 p.m. the day it aired. A police spokesman gave me a lengthy statement on how the family's 911 calls were given a low priority based on what cops knew at the time. He said there wasn't enough evidence to break in or evidence that a crime was being committed. I added the key parts of the statement, rewrote a chunk of the piece, and put the entire statement on our website.

After the story aired I didn't receive a single complaint from the police department. In fact, sources told me some police supervisors were angry that the two young, female cops who first responded to the apartment did not break in. Rosaura's grandmother said after the young woman was found murdered, she heard a police supervisor on the scene tell the two officers, "This wouldn't have happened if you handled it differently." Wow. That was something rarely said within earshot of a victim's loved one.

The lawyer later gave me dramatic police body camera video, which I used in a follow-up. There was one scene that showed a cop entering the apartment after Rosaura's body was found. With her gun drawn, the officer yells, "Tucson Police, anybody else in here?" No one was. Family members who were outside could be heard wailing and crying hysterically. I didn't use a lot of the video; it was too graphic and painful for the family.

However, the family's attorney dropped the lawsuit months later. His investigators determined Rosaura was most likely killed soon after she arrived at the apartment. I reported that. It was not only news, it was fair to the police to report the suit was being dropped and why.

I made a key point in my last report on the murder: A neighbor saw Rosaura's ex-boyfriend pulling her by her hair back into the apartment when she tried to leave.

The neighbor did not say anything or call 911.

Rosaura's mother advised, "Call 911. Yell. If he would have known that somebody was watching, he could have chickened out and let her go. If you see something, say something." The tragedy led April to start a nonprofit called Justice for Rosaura. It is aimed at helping victims of domestic violence and telling anyone who's aware of it to report it.

About a year later, in May 2019, Chief Magnus declined to be interviewed for my story about a new way police were handling park patrols.

Magnus had announced that due to the shortage of police officers, community service officers would patrol city parks. Known as "CSOs," they don't carry guns, Tasers or handcuffs. They do have collapsible batons and pepper spray.

I interviewed two retired, longtime cops who criticized the move. One was Jim Parks, the head of a police union. He said, "The concern was putting these community service officers out there that are untrained, into an environment where they can get themselves injured or, God forbid, killed."

The story included interviews with a deputy police chief and a city councilman who praised the plan. They said it was a smart use of resources, especially considering that TPD, with 820 officers, was 200 officers short due to financial problems. The cop said, "The purpose of these folks is not to enforce the law. That's what we have police officers for. The purpose of the park safety program is for these individuals to be ambassadors. If they decide that they need police resources, it's just one click away from their radio to call for an officer."

So I interviewed two guys on each side of the issue. But I also used short sound bites from two homeless men in a park. One said he and other homeless people carried more weapons than the CSOs did. The other homeless man told me, "The people that are here are hardheaded, most of them. And if they want to do something, the person [the CSO] is going to get hurt, if they don't have a badge and a gun."

When I requested an interview with Chief Magnus several days before the story ran, I was told he was "unavailable." The morning after it ran, I received a long, angry tweet from him. Part of it said:

"It was tough watching you run roughshod over a great program so many different people have worked so hard on. I think it's unfortunate that you would base your story theme on the stereotype of the homeless as dangerous (how many times could you show them with gleaming knives at Santa Rita Park?). This is a small segment of the homeless population and your portrayal of them in the parks is similar to suggesting all mentally ill people are dangerous-another sloppy and inaccurate stereotype."

Magnus ended his message saying, "Thank you for considering my feedback. Being 'hard-hitting' or a 'tough investigator,' is one thing. Setting up a false premise so you can generate fear is another. Take care."

I was extremely surprised by his tweets because I thought the story was right down the middle. Also, the sound bites from the deputy chief and councilman were much longer than those from the two homeless men. I believed a story about the new way of patrolling parks had to include interviews with a couple of people who were in the parks 24/7.

I replied to the chief's messages saying, "I totally disagree. The piece was extremely fair. I used sound bites from [Deputy Chief] Kasmar and Kozachik extolling the program." His response: "Yet your reply is completely non-responsive to my points . . . which somehow I don't find surprising. I realize it's difficult receiving critical feedback but I still appreciate you considering it. Have a good week ahead."

I felt the story spoke for itself. He apparently wanted my reply to be a longer, point-by-point defense.

What I couldn't say in the report was that I thought the plan was a good one. With TPD short at least a couple hundred patrol officers, I thought this was indeed a smart use of resources. I could have told Magnus that, but I don't think that would have mattered. If I had to do the story over again, I might have added a sound bite or two from a homeless person who thought having CSOs patrol the parks was a *good* idea. I remember thinking about that while doing the piece, but figured we already had interviews from the deputy chief and the councilman praising the plan.

A few weeks later I messaged Magnus directly, requesting an interview for another story. That report was about the police shortage and the ways TPD was recruiting new officers. It was a positive piece for the department. I even included a few seconds of a TPD public service announcement seeking recruits. I reported how to apply to be a cop and said there was detailed information about it on our station's website. Magnus didn't reply to my interview request.

This brings up a broader issue. Some police chiefs and heads of other major entities have tried forever to intimidate reporters. I've seen it everywhere I've worked, especially in smaller markets where the reporters are generally younger and less experienced. Most of Tucson's TV reporters I worked with were in their twenties and thirties. When I was their age I was intimidated by people I perceived as powerful. I was afraid to rock the boat and possibly have someone complain about me to my boss. I quickly learned from watching and talking to more experienced reporters that while I had to be fair and respectful to everyone, my main priority was our viewers, the taxpayer, the little guy.

I learned to be thick-skinned after several years in the business and that reporting isn't a popularity contest. I learned the old investigative reporter adage, to "hold the powerful accountable and give voice to the voiceless." If a public official stopped talking to me because he or she didn't like my line of questioning or how they came across in a report, so be it.

It's not just police departments. All sorts of powerful institutions, even ones many people respect, can work just as hard to be intimidating. I think the University of Arizona has intimidated the Tucson news media for years. Before at least two of my stories, a UA spokesperson asked me when they would air, then said, "Our lawyers wanted me to ask you because they'll be watching." I told him exactly when they could watch.

One UA story I wanted badly to report involved head basketball coach Sean Miller. One of our photographers was recording a game in which Miller loudly cursed out a player. This was a world-class rant caught on camera. I was watching it on ESPN, and the network's camera showed Miller screaming at the player as he removed him from the game. This was seconds before halftime, and I remember thinking, "Why didn't he wait until halftime when he could do that in the privacy of the locker room?" The network's analyst Bill Walton also said he thought the rant was a bit much.

Our new sports reporter used the clip when he showed the game highlights. At Miller's regular news conference a couple of days later, the reporter, a talented young guy named Ari Alexander, approached the coach to introduce himself. Alexander extended his hand and

Miller said, "No, I'm good" and did not extend his. Classy move. And when Ari asked a question during the news conference regarding the rant, Miller refused to answer, saying, "Next question."

A week later at Miller's news conference, he again refused to answer Ari's questions.

A guy making about $3 million a year in a high-profile job at a taxpayer-funded state university refused to answer a reporter's question because he didn't like video his station aired. Too bad, coach.

Miller's not the only big-name coach who has tried to intimidate local reporters. Their bosses, the athletic directors, need to talk to them about it, but the coach is a bigger star at the university, and the AD is often intimidated.

Ari told KVOA management about Miller's rudeness. When I heard about it I had a suggestion that I proposed to my news director. I would go to Miller's next news conference with my photographer and ask him about the rant and why he was so angry that our station showed it. People were talking about it, and Ari was 100 percent right in showing it.

I didn't go to Miller's next news conference. After the second time Miller refused to shake Ari's hand or answer his questions, our general manager called the university's athletic director and the issue was resolved. Miller answered Alexander's question at his next news conference.

Credit to our GM for sticking up for Alexander.

There's a double standard many coaches apply to network and local reporters. The only way to change that is for small-market reporters to stand up for themselves. Their bosses need to guide them. Some local news directors do not give enough guidance to young reporters. Many of these reporters need to be told when they have been soft on interviewees. They need to know they have to ask tough questions sometimes.

Even if a coach doesn't like them.

CHAPTER THIRTY-THREE

Mayor's Misguided Assistant

SOUND BITE:

"Unless he's getting some pretty explicit threats, then I don't see the justification for it."

—A Tucson councilman on the mayor using two police officers as bodyguards

Jonathan Rothschild in 2013 became the first mayor in Tucson history to have a bodyguard, and he had two. The first was assigned to work outside his office in February of that year after a suspicious package arrived at City Hall.

It turned out to be a blanket.

The second bodyguard was added to the mayor's security detail in November 2013. The officers accompanied Rothschild to and from public events. A source told me that some cops and city leaders were not happy about losing two officers from an already depleted force. Yes, it was only two cops, they acknowledged, but there were

172

hundreds fewer patrol officers than in recent years, and every officer that could be on the streets could help.

I was also told that Rothschild often used the police officers to get him his lunch, on taxpayers' time.

I learned that the police chief wanted me to report the story on the mayor's bodyguards. I thought it would be interesting reporting the pros and cons of a small-town mayor needing two bodyguards. Representative Gabby Giffords and eighteen others had been shot, six fatally, on January 8, 2011, while she held a constituents meeting outside a Tucson supermarket, so tensions over public servants being assaulted were legitimate.

I interviewed the police chief and Councilman Steve Kozachik. Like Mayor Rothschild, Kozachik was a Democrat and usually sided with him. But not on this issue, which surprised me.

Kozachik said, "We have a budget situation; we're down cops right now. We're going to lose some more perhaps later on this year when we get deeper into the budget situation. The question is what's the proper deployment for the officers, and in my opinion, it's out in the community."

Police Chief Roberto Villaseñor said the request for protection came from the mayor. The chief said he added a second cop to the detail because if someone attacks the mayor, one officer isn't enough. The chief acknowledged he had received some complaints from those who felt the mayor didn't need bodyguards. And sources told me that the chief was unhappy about the mayor having two bodyguards. But publicly he sang a different tune.

"The part that gets to me here in Tucson," Villaseñor said. "is after January 8 of 2011, we can't sit here and say that these types of events don't occur in our community."

I understood what the chief was doing. He was appointed by the mayor and council and did not want to publicly criticize them. But he sure wanted the public to know about the two bodyguards.

I called Mayor Rothschild's assistant in charge of scheduling to request an interview. She said he wasn't available during the time frame I requested, even though I provided a few different days and told her it wouldn't take long. It seemed to me it was a subject the mayor did not want to discuss. So, I checked his schedule and saw he had a speech at the Children's Museum of Tucson.

I waited in the back of the room at the museum during Rothschild's talk while my photographer got video of him. Afterwards, when Rothschild and his assistant were waiting for his car to pull up, we approached him, camera rolling. I shook his hand in my usual friendly way and told him I was there to ask questions about his bodyguards. His assistant appeared upset with me. The mayor said, "Fine, no problem."

I started the interview by asking Rothschild, "Could the officers be better used on patrol?" He said, "They would not be on patrol. They would be answering the calls, because we found that's the effective use."

Huh? I thought. *What the heck does that mean?* Rothschild explained that his bodyguards were members of an alternative response–call unit that responded to lower-priority calls. I didn't see how they could respond to any calls if they had to stay with the mayor. He had no answer for that.

I then asked the mayor, "Do you ever ask any of your security detail to get you food?" He said, "I will, when I'm out and about, stop in a restaurant—not even a restaurant, always drive-thru. I always pay for it."

I thanked Rothschild for his time and returned to the station. He did not seem upset at all. He had always been cordial to me, and he was this time.

His assistant had a different reaction.

My assignment editor told me he received a very angry call from the assistant, who claimed I "ambushed" the mayor. "Ambush" is an overused word spoken by people who don't understand the news business. Ambush is defined as "a surprise attack on someone from a concealed position." My photographer and I had calmly walked up to the mayor in plain sight. I introduced myself (I had been in Tucson a few months and we hadn't met), and I asked him if he could answer some questions.

Another phrase used by some people who know nothing about journalism is "hit piece." They use that when referring to a story they think was unfair. I have often heard people use the term for one reason: They were criticized in the piece. I always asked anyone who complained about any of my stories, "Was anything I reported inaccurate?"

The mayor's bodyguards' story included an interview with a professor in the University of Arizona's School of Government and Public Policy. Mike Polakowski said, "We live in the wild, wild, wild West, where people are able to carry guns just about everywhere." He thought the mayor was right in wanting two bodyguards. "We ought to be able to afford our public officials some level of protection," the professor said.

Almost exactly three years after the story ran, Mayor Rothschild was carjacked at gunpoint. It happened outside his home on a Saturday morning. The mayor was not hurt and his city-owned car was found a few blocks away.

His bodyguards were not with him at the time.

CHAPTER THIRTY-FOUR

Horrendous Housing

SOUND BITE:

"I don't think we have to live like this. It's horrible."

—Leslye Griffin, a tenant in a public housing building

My favorite and most gratifying stories were those that led to positive changes. People who say the news media does only negative stories are either not paying attention or just anti-media. I did plenty of positive pieces. I did one in 2016 that created a stir within my station.

A woman named Leslye Griffin called to tell me about numerous problems in her apartment building near downtown Tucson. The Coronado housed forty-one apartments for low-income residents and was funded by the Department of Housing and Urban Development. A local company, Werth Realty, had been the property manager for six months. Werth was also an advertiser on KVOA. I proceeded with the story because advertisers were not my concern. Advertisers worked with the sales department.

Leslye gave my photographer and me a tour of the building. The

176

Coronado was built in 1928 and was listed on the National Register of Historic Places. It looked prehistoric. We saw exposed wires and pipes and broken light bulbs in hallways. There was a large hole in a hallway ceiling. Carpets contained dog and cat feces, vomit and urine stains. There was a dangerously loose stair railing. The lock on the building's entry door was broken. Leslye said, "I'm extremely angry because I fear for my safety. I sleep with a rubber mallet under my bed."

Leslye and several other residents said they had been reporting the problems to Werth Realty for months and few repairs were made. Leslye claimed her phone calls to Werth were not returned.

I interviewed the property manager for Werth. She said, "When somebody calls in and reports repairs, then we take care of them right away." I followed that up by asking her, "Would you want to live here?" She replied, "Uh, um, I would . . . I didn't . . . if it was cleaned up, yeah I would."

At my request, Werth sent me proof of repair jobs it had done, twenty-one pages of completed work orders. But from the mess I had seen, the company had a lot more work to do. The city agreed.

I interviewed the director of Tucson's Housing and Community Development Department, which oversaw Werth Realty's compliance with the federal HUD contract. Sally Stang said, "They're the property manager. They should be at that building every day." I asked her, "Are you disappointed in Werth?" She said, "Absolutely. We're definitely going to talk to them."

The morning after we told Stang about the building's problems, three teams of inspectors from Housing and Code Enforcement showed up there, six men total. Stang said they found twenty-three items that failed HUD's quality standards. "Those are all things that are just unacceptable items that should have been noticed by management," Stang said.

I again interviewed the property manager. She said, "We've already got the work orders in, my maintenance guys are up, already trying to fix the hole. I've got the carpets scheduled to be cleaned."

Within twenty-four hours of the inspectors informing Werth about the items that failed quality standards, everything was repaired. A new lock was installed on the front door and the carpets were cleaned. I reported all of that in a follow-up piece. Leslye said, "I think that it's incredible that it took the news to get everything fixed."

After the second piece ran, my news director told me the station's general manager wanted to see me and to bring my scripts. When I entered the GM's office, the sales manager was also there. He was a good guy but was obviously displeased that I reported on a client. The sales manager wanted me to do another piece on how Werth quickly fixed the problems. I said tenants complained to Werth for months and the repairs were made only *after* our report. I told him I already reported that Werth fixed everything. The general manager had a copy of the script stating exactly that. To the GM's credit, I was not ordered to do a third piece.

Werth then pulled its ads from the station. KVOA lost thousands of dollars.

The salesman who had the account ignored me when we passed each other in the station and never talked to me again. I understood his anger, but we had different agendas. I wanted to help viewers; he wanted to sell commercials.

About a year later, I heard that Werth was back advertising on the station.

CHAPTER THIRTY-FIVE

Off-Key Owner

SOUND BITE:

"He could sell the damn underwear off Mother Teresa if she were alive."

—Marie Russell, a disgruntled former customer of a music store, about the shop's owner

In the hundreds of stories I've done on bad businesses, I thought some owners were just incompetent, but others were fraudulent. I thought the owner of a Tucson music store was, at the very least, the former, and at worst, the latter.

Arizona's attorney general said the guy was committing fraud.

I first received complaints from viewers in early 2016 about Sticks n' Strings, a longtime store that sold new musical instruments and used ones on consignment.

A twenty-nine-year-old guitarist named Gabriel Wright told me he bought a cabinet speaker from the store for $300. He was stunned at what happened soon after he took it home. "When I opened the cabinet that Tony sold me, that's when I see that he had put in speakers that basically cost about twelve dollars at Walmart," Wright said.

"Tony" was Tony Bernard, the owner of Sticks n' Strings. Customers told me his father ran the store beautifully for thirty years, but that Tony had a different approach.

Several former customers told the attorney general and me that Bernard took tens of thousands of dollars for instruments that were not delivered, and when they asked for their money back, Tony gave them excuses. Former customers said he would either not give refunds or take weeks to provide them. Some angry customers would show up at the store with a couple of friends acting as bodyguards because they said Tony had a temper and would kick them out of the place. Customers claimed Tony would blame the instrument's manufacturer for the delays. Other complaints lodged with the attorney general's office were about instruments customers had given Tony on consignment. They said when he sold the piece, he wouldn't tell them and would pocket the money instead of giving them their share, usually around 70 percent.

An amateur guitar player named George Russell said he and his wife Marie had paid Bernard more than $11,000 for guitars and related equipment. They were senior citizens who didn't live near the store and didn't want to drive there often to demand refunds. They were also very patient with Bernard. "We've got one guitar that we've had on order for about three years now," George said. Three years! Obviously, something was off-key at the music store.

After receiving these complaints and others, I read more complaints on the Better Business Bureau's website. The BBB had given Sticks n' Strings an *F* rating. I interviewed the BBB spokesperson, who said the agency had reached out to Bernard "multiple times with these complaints and he has failed to respond to any of them."

The *F* rating wasn't Bernard's biggest problem.

While I was transcribing the interviews and getting prepared to call Bernard to try to get his explanation, the investigative producer who sat next to me at work, a terrific newsman named

Paul Birmingham, found out that Arizona attorney general Mark Byrnovich just two days earlier charged Sticks n' Strings with consumer fraud.

I immediately called the AG's spokesperson. He confirmed the legal action and sent me a copy of the filing. The suit said Bernard "requested and accepted consumers' payments for merchandise it [the store] never ordered, delivered or provided a refund for." The suit requested that Bernard make restitution to customers, pay the state up to $10,000 for each alleged violation, and stop accepting pre-payments for products unless they were immediately available for shipping.

I now had to make a decision. Should I call Bernard to request an interview or just show up at the store? I thought that with all the information I had, Bernard would refuse an interview. I had been told by several customers who knew Bernard that he would not agree to an interview if I asked him over the phone. They said he often avoided their calls. I figured if he was avoiding customers, he would certainly not take a call from a reporter who was investigating him.

Early in my career I was too afraid to show up unannounced to question anyone with the camera rolling. So, I usually ended up with nothing. The person I was investigating would send out a colleague to tell me he or she was unavailable, to leave my card, and that they'd call me. They rarely called and I would have no video.

I showed up at Sticks n' Strings with the AG's lawsuit in my hands and my photographer rolling.

A young woman behind the counter said Bernard was in the back room and she told him we were there. He came out a few minutes later. I didn't ask him if we could do an interview. I just jumped right in. I showed him the attorney general's lawsuit, and he claimed, "I don't know much about this right now but if . . . we can get back to you on it?" I replied, "Sure, take your time." I was surprised he didn't know he was being sued, much less by the most powerful attorney in the state.

Bernard walked away from me towards his back office, reading the lawsuit. He said in a low but audible voice, "Oh my God." So maybe he really didn't know about it, because he appeared shaken.

Bernard returned to the counter a few minutes later, appearing extremely nervous. He denied altering Gabriel Wright's speaker cabinet, although Wright was technically oriented and was certain the expensive speaker had been replaced by a cheap one. Regarding the other complaints, I told Bernard, "There's a constant thread in all these complaints, both from the state and the people we interviewed, that you do a stall job. You delay, you keep blaming manufacturers. You tell customers, 'It's not in, it's not in', and you take customers' money and you do something else with it. But you do not deliver the product for months, if ever."

Bernard replied, "I know it seems that way, but that's the thing. We're waiting for the stuff to come in from the companies and a lot of stuff is from overseas and we always say, 'Do you want to change to something different that's available?' And most of them are like, 'No, we'll just wait for it.'"

Bernard later called the complaints "misunderstandings," and said, "We're trying to set up procedures to make sure this never happens again." Some complaints were years old, and only after I questioned him did Bernard say he's "trying to set up procedures."

Sometimes I heard from people involved in stories months after they aired because they didn't see it live but found it online. Eight months later, I received a call from another angry customer.

Joe Bucci was a guitar player in a duo. He bought a graphite guitar from Sticks n' Strings for $2,800 in February 2016. Bucci said Bernard told him he'd order it from the manufacturer and it would be in the store soon. But five weeks later, after Bucci called Bernard several times for updates, he became suspicious. He called the manufacturer directly and was told the guitar was never ordered.

I then called the manufacturer. Its owner said Bernard called him just a few days earlier to order Bucci's guitar, but the order was refused. The owner said Bernard owed him a lot of money and the company stopped taking his orders.

Bucci said, "How he remains in business is mind-boggling to me." He also told me he gave Bernard several items to sell on consignment. He said Bernard paid him $175 for an amplifier. "I get down there, I pick up the check. The check bounces," he said.

Bucci said he gave Bernard a Fender guitar to sell on consignment seven months earlier. He claimed Bernard told him he could get $1,400 for it, but Bernard sold the guitar and kept Bucci's percentage, $980.

I called Bernard and told him I was doing a follow-up piece about Bucci's complaints. Minutes later, Bucci called me. He said Bernard told him he would give him his cut that same day. We arranged to meet Bucci outside Sticks n' Strings.

Bucci said, "He gave me a thousand dollars, twenty dollars more than what he owed me for my troubles." He showed us the cash, on camera. A true "money shot."

So, for eight months Bernard didn't pay Bucci. Then when Bernard found out we were doing a story on it, he paid him the same day.

Bucci said, "There's no question why he decided to do it. It's because you're here. Thank you so much for what you do for those of us. There's not enough consumer protection left in the whole country, so I'm glad we've got you guys."

I felt great for Joe Bucci but wanted the other customers to get their money back.

In 2019, a spokesperson for the AG told me that Bernard was making his restitution payments on schedule. I hoped he would pay everyone back and turn his business around.

CHAPTER THIRTY-SIX

Dubious Donations

SOUND BITE:

"I don't like the idea that they get to choose where this extra money goes."

—Barbara Wolfe, Pima County taxpayer, on county supervisors donating taxpayers' money to outside groups

One part of an investigative reporter's job is to pressure politicians to enact positive change while informing taxpayers of questionable activities. I was pleased that a story I did in 2015 accomplished both.

I received a tip that four of the five Pima County supervisors were giving taxpayer money to their favorite outside groups without taxpayers' knowledge. County residents were already upset with the supervisors. The county had the highest property tax rate in Arizona (and terrible pothole-filled roads, but that's another story, and I reported it often). Pima was the only southern Arizona county that allowed supervisors to donate tax dollars from their annual $400,000 office budgets to their favorite organizations. In other counties, leftover money from office budgets went to capital improvement funds, which can be used to fix, say, potholes.

For roughly twenty years Pima County supervisors gave their unspent office funds to whatever groups they chose. Taxpayers had no say in the matter, and until my investigation not many were aware of it. There was no vote or public discussion. Some might construe donations as vote-buying and conflicts of interest.

After I received the tip, I checked a website called Open Books Arizona, the state's official transparency site. Two supervisors had handed out almost $90,000 over the previous two years. Richard Elias gave thousands to Planned Parenthood of Southern Arizona, which had one of his staff members on its board. He also donated to a social services agency where he used to work. He spent hundreds on a table at an event for a group he favored. Supervisor Sharon Bronson donated to numerous groups, including the Southern Arizona AIDS Foundation, a high school district and a community center. These all might be worthy causes, but that wasn't the point.

Jared Blanchard, an attorney with the Goldwater Institute, a conservative think tank based in Phoenix, told me, "This seems to be a unique feature of Pima County board members. It's a bad public policy, and it appears to be illegal. That taxpayers' money is for a specific purpose, and that is to serve the community. It is not to serve special interests that the board may favor."

Barbara Wolfe lived in Elias's district. She called Elias's donations "unconscionable." Wolfe said, "That's a choice that individuals should be able to make. If I want to give money to Planned Parenthood, that should be my choice."

Another county resident, Alex Bissett, an eighty-one-year-old living on a fixed income, said, "We're angry because it's taxpayers' money. If they spent it on the roads, I would cheer. But the roads sit there, with the potholes. They never get fixed." I asked Bissett, "If you could talk to the supervisors about these donations, what would you say?" He replied, "One word: stop."

Supervisors Elias and Bronson declined my interview requests, so I knew the best way to question them would be at a Board of

Supervisors meeting. With a crowd of voters watching, politicians usually don't walk away from reporters without commenting.

I approached Elias during a meeting recess. I said, "Explain to me why you think this is okay." He said, "Because there's a legitimate return and a public service offered to people. Folks who live in my district are low income in many cases and have significant needs." I asked Elias about his staffer also serving on the Planned Parenthood board. "You see any conflict of interest in that?" I asked. "No, absolutely not," he said. "He receives no pecuniary reward to being on that board of directors."

I also approached Supervisor Bronson during the recess. "That's taxpayers' dollars," I told her. "Yes," she said, "to agencies in need."

The supervisors did not agree with my belief, or that of the attorney at the Goldwater Institute, that when tax dollars are involved, taxpayers must have input. The attorney said he was considering a lawsuit against the county.

Two months after my report aired, the board unanimously approved a policy that would disallow unilaterally donating money directly from their office budgets to outside groups.

CHAPTER THIRTY-SEVEN

The FBI Tapes

SOUND BITE:

"I've been crucified."

—Emanuel "Book" Richardson, former University of Arizona assistant basketball coach, in a phone call with me days before he went to prison

It was college basketball's off-season, but Emanuel "Book" Richardson was busy.

The forty-four-year-old assistant coach at the University of Arizona was sitting in an office in Princeton, New Jersey, on July 20, 2017. He was talking to two guys who told him they worked for a fledgling pro sports agent. The agent was a twenty-six-year-old street hustler from Michigan named Christian Dawkins. Dawkins wanted Richardson and other college coaches to steer their star players to his firm. A player who made the NBA would make millions, and Dawkins would get a percentage. First, the coaches had to get high school studs to attend their schools of higher learning.

Coach Richardson was thought of by many UA players as a father figure looking out for their best interests. Dawkins' main target in Tucson was DeAndre Ayton, a six-feet, eleven-inch, 250-pound high school all-American. Coach Richardson did land Ayton, who

187

attended UA for one season. He would be the number one pick in the 2018 NBA draft, and his rookie salary was eight million. Agents of NBA players generally receive 4 percent commission. The agent who would eventually sign Ayton would make $320,000 a year, not including endorsement money.

Coach Richardson had no clue that one guy at that 2017 meeting was an FBI agent wearing a hidden camera.

FBI agent Jeff D'Angelo gave Richardson an envelope while saying, "That's the fifteen there." D'Angelo was referring to $15,000 in cash. Coach Richardson took it and said, "It better help with the kids." The plan was for Richardson to give the money to players, but as he would admit later, he kept it himself.

The undercover video became key evidence in Coach Richardson's case, which was part of a college basketball bribery scandal involving six other assistant coaches nationwide. The FBI also had numerous wiretapped phone calls in which Coach Richardson was heard talking about bribes with undercover agents. Before the July meeting in Princeton, he had taken a bribe of $5,000.

Coach Richardson faced a long prison sentence and considered the overwhelming evidence against him. He made a deal with prosecutors and in 2019 pleaded guilty to one count of felony bribery. He had no prior criminal record and was sentenced to three months in prison.

The audio recordings were played on television stations around the country. But I had never seen the video of Richardson taking the cash envelope from the FBI agent, and it was not previously shown by any Tucson TV station. I wanted it bad.

I called the public information officer at the US Attorney's Office for the Southern District of New York. I assumed she would ask that I file a public records request, which meant it could take weeks before I received the video. Richardson would be reporting to a federal prison in Upstate New York in a week. The story would be timelier if it aired before then.

Within ten minutes, the media liaison emailed me ninety-one files that prosecutors used as evidence in Coach Richardson's trial. They included the wiretapped phone calls and several videos, including the one showing him taking the cash. I was ecstatic. I wished every media liaison would be so quick and cooperative. It took more time getting even the simplest answers from the Tucson Police Department's public information officers.

I spent most of the next two days transcribing the video and audio files and reading court transcripts. I also wanted an interview with Coach Richardson. Other than a brief statement outside the courthouse after sentencing, Richardson hadn't given any interviews and turned down dozens of requests.

Then I thought for sure he was about to give me his first one.

One of my contacts in Tucson was a defense attorney named Brick Storts. He was eighty-three years old, dressed impeccably, and gave good interviews with colorful sound bites. Months before Richardson was scheduled to report to prison in July 2019, I began calling Storts, requesting (and begging for) an interview with his now infamous client. I called Storts every week. Five days before Richardson was to be locked up, he agreed to talk to me, based on Storts' recommendation.

There's an old saying in journalism and other businesses, "Under-sell and over-deliver." I told no one about the scheduled interview except my news director and photographer. I was concerned about Coach Richardson getting cold feet and canceling.

On Friday, July 12, we were set up at 11 a.m. in Storts' office. When Richardson hadn't shown by 11:30, Storts called him. Richardson said he was at home, being delayed by federal agents who were taking inventory of his assets. He said he didn't think it would take so long and rescheduled the interview for 4 p.m.

Richardson again failed to show. When I returned to the newsroom, he called me and apologized. He also said the FBI's case was "the tip of the iceberg" and that many other college coaches were taking bribes and just hadn't been caught. I believed him, considering the pressure on coaches at major programs to win and the need for money that so many high school players have. He called his sentence "unfair", considering the good deeds he had done throughout his life, his mentoring of countless young people. He agreed to do the interview the following Monday.

The next day Richardson sent me this text: "Matthew, after talking things over with my family, I will not do any interviews before I do my 90 days. When I'm done with my 90 days I will sit down with you and only YOU to talk about my whole process in its entirety. I have no problem staying in touch with you during these next 90 days and when I get out coming to sit down with you in a nice location where I can decompress and tell my story. I'm going to help you because I believe you do an awesome job. I will write you and please know I'm only doing this for you!!!!!!!"

My report aired the night before Richardson reported to prison. It started with the video of him taking the cash-filled envelope. I included a few more FBI undercover videos, some wiretapped phone calls of him talking about taking bribes, and an interview with his lawyer. There had been great speculation that Richardson's longtime boss, the aforementioned head basketball coach Sean Miller, knew about and was involved in the bribes. Miller consistently and vehemently denied any wrongdoing, and I included his one public statement about it. While I was disappointed about not interviewing with Richardson, I thought it was a solid piece.

After Richardson got out of prison in October 2019 I texted him and he quickly called me. He said he needed time to think about doing an interview. He implied that he needed to get paid but didn't come right out and ask for money. It's called "checkbook journalism," and our station didn't pay for interviews. Richardson stopped returning my texts and calls and didn't give me the interview he said he would before entering prison.

During our phone call days before he was incarcerated, I asked Richardson why he took bribes when he was making $250,000 a year. He said, "I needed money to pay medical bills for a family member." He also told me he wanted to coach again in college someday.

PART IV

You Didn't Ask Me But ...

CHAPTER THIRTY-EIGHT

Characters

I've worked with some memorable characters. The one who stands out the most is Lloyd Lindsay Young. Lloyd was the wackiest weatherman I've ever seen.

One of Lloyd's on-air trademarks was the way he began every forecast. He would yell long and loud, "*Hellooooo*" to a different city. One night it would be "*Hellooooo, Hoboken.*" The next it might be "*Hellooooo, Ho-Ho-Kus,*" or whatever city was requested as a mention by a viewer. He'd take five seconds to say "*Hellooooo.*" Station management made him stop yelling "*Hellooooo*" in June 1995. I thought then that management was soon going to tell Lloyd goodbye.

Starting his forecasts without yelling "*Hellooooo*" was so noticeable the *New York Times* reported it. Lloyd told the paper, "They're afraid it may offend too many viewers. They're afraid that there's some small minority of people out there who don't want to be yelled at. They've done that before; the last time was six years ago. I just try to roll with the punches."

Lloyd didn't have a meteorologist degree, and viewers didn't care. He was hilarious, but during bad weather he did no shtick.

He had loved weather since he was a kid growing up in Hollywood, California, and was very knowledgeable. We became friends and Lloyd often told me, "Weather just turns me on."

When Lloyd changed the graphics on the weather wall behind him, he yelled, "*Science!*" I saw him say it a thousand times, yet I laughed every time. We remain in touch and I begin every phone call with Lloyd by yelling "*Science!*" He used props to point to places on the map of the US. Some of his pointers included a mannequin's leg, a seventy-five-pound artillery shell, and an icicle. The most outrageous was used one night when Lloyd worked in Evansville, Indiana. He had a stripper in a bikini stand on her head and used her high heel shoes as pointers. I kid you not. His antics were clearly over the top for some viewers, which he acknowledged, but they were in the minority.

Lloyd's big break is one of those Hollywood-type stories. He was doing weather in the small market of Idaho Falls. The general manager of a San Francisco station was at a ski resort in Sun Valley with his teenaged sons. The GM wanted to hit the slopes, but his kids had seen Lloyd previously from their hotel room and said, "Wait, Dad, we have to watch this weatherman." The GM watched, too. Lloyd was soon hired by KGO-TV. He moved from market number 164 to market 5. He told me his salary tripled.

Lloyd became so popular in New York that the comedian George Carlin had him open one of his HBO specials with his trademark "*Hellooooo.*" Years before Bill Cosby's reputation was ruined, he called the Channel 9 newsroom and asked Lloyd to do the weather from his New York apartment, and Lloyd did it.

Lloyd was fired by Channel 9 in 1995 not long after the station ordered him to stop yelling "*Hellooooo.*" He said he believes it was simply because he was making too much money. I agree. I couldn't see any other reason our most popular on-air personality and one of the most recognizable in the New York market was let go. Lloyd's son, George, who did the weekend weather and weekday reporting at Channel 9, quit in protest. Ballsy move by George.

I worked in New York another seven years, and viewers often asked me what happened to Lloyd. Even when I worked in Tampa years later, transplanted New Yorkers or visitors who saw me in public and remembered me from New York would ask about Lloyd.

Lloyd and I remain friends. He and his wife visited me in Tucson in 2019. He called me a month later and began the conversation in an unusually serious tone. "Matt, I have some bad news that I am only telling a few friends," he said. "Doctors found a tumor in my brain." Naturally, I was stunned.

Lloyd said his doctor was 90 percent certain the tumor was benign. Of course, you worry about the other 10 percent, and Lloyd was worried.

Lloyd underwent brain surgery on June 15, 2019. The tumor was benign and he's fine today. I was in touch with Lloyd and his wife soon after the surgery. He then posted the good news on Facebook and told me to share it here.

Channel 9 was the wildest TV station to work at in the New York market in the late '80s and early '90s. Howard Stern, Matt Lauer, and Morton Downey Jr. hosted shows produced in our Secaucus studio. The circus had come to Secaucus.

Stern had the most successful radio show in history when Channel 9 hired him and sidekick Robin Quivers for a Saturday night TV program. The self-proclaimed "King of All Media" had a reported budget for production and salary of $100,000 a show. I was still a general assignment reporter in 1990 and was assigned to interview Howard and Robin the day before the show debuted. My news report was a plug, a free commercial for the show. I knew the deal but couldn't refuse the assignment, and besides, I wanted to meet Howard and Robin. I was and remain a fan. They were extremely likable.

One Stern show bit was memorable, especially for us in the news department. Our assistant news director had become the executive producer of Stern's TV show. In the bit he played a dog. He got on all fours, wore a collar, and barked.

This was the guy who recently was the number two news executive, acting like he had to do number one—on TV. He was a smart newsman, but I thought he lowered himself, in more ways than one. At least it made for some good humor for a while. Some of my colleagues periodically walked around the newsroom barking. The dog act didn't hurt the guy professionally. He has had a long and successful career in news management.

Morton Downey Jr.'s show debuted on Channel 9 in 1987 and was immediately called trash TV by critics. It made Jerry Springer's show look like *Masterpiece Theatre.* It was also a hit.

Downey was a staunch conservative and chain-smoker who screamed at guests and blew smoke in their faces when he disagreed with them. His fans were known as loudmouths. The show had a live studio audience, and the audience members entering the station looked like the same crowd that went to fake wrestling matches. And there were fights during Downey's shows, though usually forced, if not staged.

Viewers quickly tired of the noise and Downey's over-the-top antics. His big early ratings declined by 1989. Channel 9 moved his time slot from 9 p.m. to 12:30 a.m. In late April 1989, Downey claimed he was attacked in a San Francisco airport bathroom by neo-Nazis. He said they painted swastikas on his face and tried to shave his head.

The swastikas were still there two days later when I interviewed Downey in his Trump Tower apartment. The problems with his story were that the swastikas were painted on backwards, as though

Downey put them on himself while looking in a mirror. Police found no suspects or evidence of an attack. An airport spokesman told me, "The facts certainly did not happen the way Mr. Downey said they happened. We cannot substantiate any of his claims." That prompted speculation that Downey wanted attention because his show wasn't getting much of it anymore. I asked him repeatedly if he painted the swastikas on himself and he denied it.

The Morton Downey Jr. Show was canceled in July 1989. It lasted less than two years. Downey died in 2001 from lung cancer.

I worked at the same station as Matt Lauer did, twice. The first time was in 1981. I was a reporter at WXEX-TV in Richmond and he co-hosted a syndicated entertainment show called *PM Magazine.* (Like me, Lauer attended Ohio University; he quit before graduation to take a broadcasting job in West Virginia.) We worked together again eight years later. While I was reporting for Channel 9, Lauer co-hosted a three-hour live interview program called *9 Broadcast Plaza.* That was the station's address, but it wasn't Lauer's for long. He refused to do live advertisements for a mattress company. He also disliked the tabloid turn the show had taken. I admired Matt's position

I did not admire his position in 2017. He was fired from his co-host job on the *Today* show for alleged "inappropriate sexual behavior in the workplace." He reportedly was making $21 million a year.

Channel 9's terrific longtime anchorwoman Sara Lee Kessler read the sports on the station's newscasts every Monday at noon because our sports director was off. Producer Allen Levine had some

fun with that, unbeknownst to Sara Lee. Allen always put a golf story in Monday newscasts so Sara Lee would have to say *putts*. Except Allen wrote so it could be construed as *putz*, which derives from the Yiddish word for penis. Not the most mature joke, I know. But a nice break from the daily grind and tragic stories.

Allen would write, "Tiger Woods had trouble with his putts." The newsroom would be silent as we waited for it. Co-anchor Van Hackett sat next to Sara Lee and had to suppress laughter. Allen would put "putts" in golf stories two or three times.

When the sports guy moved on to another job, a gag tape was shown at his goodbye party. Levine put in a golf clip he had written, in which Sara Lee said of a golfer, "He weighs 300 pounds, but he's a wizard with his putts." Sara Lee finally got the joke, and was a good sport about it.

There was a young reporter at WWOR who took mistakes very hard. After he felt he did a bad live shot or stumbled during a live in-studio piece, he'd walk to a side hallway and bang his head against the wall. Several bangs, and not gently. He'd do this while mumbling to himself, "Stupid, stupid, stupid." I felt bad for him, putting that much pressure on himself.

Another Channel 9 colleague didn't bang his head against the wall; he banged out stories. Bob Miller was a veteran New York reporter. Photographers nicknamed him "The Hammer" because of how quickly he hammered out his reports. Bob was an old-school, "just the facts, ma'am" type. He knew what he wanted from interviewees, and most of his interviews consisted of no more than two questions. He felt that was all he needed for a ninety-second story, so why take more time in the field and have more tape to screen while on deadline? Some of Bob's interviews even consisted of only one question. And one question was all he needed one night to create a memorable moment.

On the night in 1990 when mob boss John Gotti was found not guilty of assault and conspiracy charges, he returned home to an illogical hero's welcome in his Queens, New York, neighborhood. He was smiling as he walked from his car to his house, leading a large crowd of friends, family, and reporters.

Gotti publicly claimed for years he wasn't in the Mafia, that he had a legitimate job in the plumbing supply business. Gotti ignored reporters' questions until Bob asked, "So, now that your trial is over, when are you going to return to your plumbing supply business?" Gotti couldn't keep a straight face. He stopped, turned towards Bob, and smiled. Even the usually stone-faced mafioso had to acknowledge Bob's sense of humor.

I have a type A personality. I suppose I inherited it from my mother. A photographer I worked with in New York was a type triple-A. Bruce Martin was frenetic almost all the time. When driving to a big breaking news story, instead of sitting in heavy New York traffic, Bruce *drove on sidewalks. In the middle of the city.* He made sure no pedestrians were in his path. I confess I never told him to stop doing that. He was also a terrific photographer. In our twenty years of working together, he never made a technical mistake that caused us to lose a shot. Bruce had a good heart and was so passionate about his craft, he brought two cameras to every shoot in case one malfunctioned. He's the only photographer I worked with who did that.

Channel 5 in Cleveland had a cast of on-air characters who worked there for years and were local celebrities. One was sports director Gib Shanley. He was a chain-smoker; you could smoke in newsrooms in those days and a lot of us did. Gib was a cranky but likable middle-aged guy. He was also the longtime radio voice of the NFL's Cleveland Browns. He was the most popular sports anchor in the city. I found out how popular when I heard about a controversial incident involving Gib before I worked there.

During the Iranian hostage crisis in 1979, some Iranian students in Cleveland burned an American flag. At the end of Gib's sportscast that night, he said, "I know this isn't sports, but I'm going to do it anyway." He then held up an Iranian flag, took out his cigarette lighter, set the flag on fire, and threw it to the floor. He said if that offended anyone, they should leave the country.

Management was not happy. The news director told Gib his action was unprofessional. Management crafted a statement for Gib to read on the air. He said, "It was not the brightest thing I ever did." The flag-burning made national news, and I heard that, privately, station executives were pleased about the attention. They wouldn't admit that publicly because it would be politically incorrect.

The day after the incident, 200 people marched through downtown's Public Square in support of Shanley. They held up signs saying, "GIB'S GOT GUTS." When I met Gib two years later and asked him about the flag-burning, he said he was glad he did it.

Many years later he told the *Cleveland Plain Dealer* the incident was blown out of proportion, adding, "But I suppose I would do it again."

Gib was also a man-about-town. I met a beautiful woman who worked as a cashier in a grocery store near my apartment and asked her out. She said yes and gave me her phone number. Before our date, Gib approached me in the newsroom and said he dated her previously. He was almost twice her age, but hey, that was a perk of being a local celebrity. The woman called Gib to make sure I was single. Gib informed her I was and gave her his stamp of approval. He was a good colleague.

Dorothy Fuldheim was another colleague in Cleveland. She was a legend, called the "First Lady of Television News," and credited with being the first woman in the US to anchor a television news broadcast. She interviewed everyone from Hitler and Mussolini to Helen Keller and Martin Luther King Jr.

When I met Dorothy in 1981, she was still doing commentaries during WEWS newscasts. She was eighty-seven years old and sometimes disoriented. At the end of numerous commentaries, Dorothy didn't wait for a commercial break or taped piece to leave the set. She simply got up and walked behind the anchors while they were reading the next story. The anchors had trouble keeping a straight face as Dorothy walked behind them.

Dorothy was a brilliant woman and I admired her tremendously. She grew up not far from me in New Jersey and called me into her office a few times to discuss her upbringing. I didn't want to talk about New Jersey; I wanted to hear about her career. To my surprise, she paid attention to my reports and often complimented me on them. That meant a lot because Dorothy was a tough woman who did not give false praise. I was fortunate to have known her during my two years in Cleveland. In 1989 I was driving to work in New York and heard on the radio that Dorothy died at the age of ninety-six. I thought of our talks in her office and tears came to my eyes.

Al Roker, a star for twenty-five years on the *Today* show, was the weatherman at WKYC in Cleveland when I worked at WEWS. One Saturday morning our stations opposed each other in a game of touch football. It was supposed to be just for fun.

There was a large crowd of news viewers in attendance. This was years before Al had gastric bypass surgery, and he was still heavy. My teammate who was covering Al was a photographer and usually a mellow guy. But when Al got behind him and caught a long pass, my teammate jumped on Al's back and tackled him. In a touch football game.

Al came up swinging. He yelled, "What the hell was that?" He was justified for being angry. There was an ensuing shoving match between Al and my teammate. It was not a good look for the fans who watched us nightly. Years later when I was working in New York I ran into Al while I was working on a story near NBC. We laughed about the skirmish in that otherwise touch football game.

I knew two fascinating and famous mayors named Ed. Ed Hanna was the first politician I ever covered. The longtime mayor of Utica, New York, was always colorful and sometimes acted crazy. According to critics, he was also corrupt.

Hanna was the city's first independent mayor in eighty-eight years when he was elected in 1973. I met him in 1977 during my first reporting job when he was seeking reelection. He cursed me out privately a few times during one-on-one interviews when he didn't like my questions. I've never covered any elected official since then who dropped f-bombs to my face. I was twenty-three and new at this, but asked him some tough questions that would provoke colorful answers. My editor might have to bleep over a few words, but Hanna's salty language was part of who he was and I thought viewers should see that.

Hanna was on *60 Minutes* once and didn't curb his cursing for its large national audience. The interview contained numerous bleeps. His interviews were usually must-see TV because you didn't know if he was going to go on a rant or what his mood was that day. He could be angry or quite friendly and funny. He had a raspy voice and sounded like he had a permanent case of laryngitis. He was a short, thin, quick-talking, quick-walking guy with a funny gait that made it seem like he was shuffling.

Hanna was a self-made millionaire who perfected the technique used in coin-operated photo booths. He took a mayoral salary of one dollar a year. Residents loved or loathed him. His supporters said he was a regular guy, a populist who worked tirelessly for the little guy. Critics said he misused federal funds and wasted money on his pet beautification projects. He ordered construction of what he named the "Tower of Hope" outside City Hall to honor Bob Hope. The famous comedian had no particular connection to Utica. Hanna just liked him.

Hanna built a park next to City Hall, using more than 400,000 taxpayers' dollars. It was originally called Terrace Park but Hanna had it renamed Edward A. Hanna Park. This was although the federal government prohibited using federal funds for a building named after a living person. You had to be dead.

Hanna also put his name on plaques and monuments. The city was audited by the feds over the way it used more than $1.3 million in federal funds between 1997 and 1998. It had to be paid back.

Hanna's critics called him an embarrassment to the city. He once said at a news conference, "I am the mayor of a lousy city," and advised its young residents to leave. The comments got him in the *New York Times* and on an ABC network news report by Harry Reasoner. Hanna loved the attention. He was elected mayor four times between 1974 and 2000. He frequently fought with the news media and at various times told his staff not to talk to reporters. The local newspaper, the *Observer-Dispatch,* called Hanna "a demagogue and a bully."

Yet in 1999, Hanna was reelected mayor with 75 percent of the vote. In 2000, four former employees, all men, filed federal lawsuits against Hanna and the city, citing sexual harassment. The city settled their claims for $250,000, but Hanna never admitted any wrongdoing.

In 2007 when Hanna was eighty-five years old and seeking reelection, he wanted to prove he was fit to hold office again. So he did jumping jacks at a public event. What reporter wouldn't love getting that on camera?

Hanna died in early 2009 at eighty-six years old. He had requested that upon his death, three songs be played over a loudspeaker in the Tower of Hope: "Over the Rainbow," "The Impossible Dream," and "My Way." When he died, the songs played all day.

I met Ed Koch in 1983. He was New York's mayor from 1978 to 1989 and a quintessential New Yorker. "I'm just a Jewish kid from the Bronx," he often said. His trademark greeting to people on the street was, "How am I doin'?" He could be thin-skinned and arrogant. He always acted as though he thought he was the smartest guy in the room. But he was smart and I enjoyed interviewing him. He loved doing interviews and sparring with reporters; the sessions were never boring and often hilarious.

When asked about groups that criticized him, unlike most politicians Koch didn't give politically correct answers. He called good government panels "elitists," some black and Hispanic leaders "poverty pimps." He once called neighborhood protestors "crazies" and Representative Bella Abzug "wacko." Years later Koch described New York mayor Rudy Giuliani as "a good mayor but a terrible person."

Koch had a high-pitched, whiny voice and a New York accent. He would often end interviews with a stinging statement aimed at an adversary. He would do it with a smile on his face while looking directly into the camera. I frequently had to restrain myself from laughing.

After Koch was defeated by David Dinkins in the 1989 Democratic primary when seeking a fourth term, he told me, "The people just got tired of me." He was right, I thought. He went on to several jobs on TV and radio. He was an avid moviegoer and became a film critic. He was an attorney and worked at a law firm, largely as a figurehead. That's where I continued to interview him to get his colorful opinions on the latest New York political developments. He remained accessible; I can't recall him turning down any of my interview requests.

Koch died in 2013 of congestive heart failure at the age of eighty-eight. The *New York Times* posted on its website a 2007 video interview with him. The video ended with Koch saying, "I want to be remembered as being a proud Jew who loved the people of the City of New York and did his best to make their lives better."

CHAPTER THIRTY-NINE

In Harm's Way

SOUNDBITE:

"Daddy!"

—The infant son of a man killed on 9/11 when he saw him in family videos

I cried twice while doing stories. The first was when I was covering the New Jersey Special Olympics in the late '80s. I watched these kids run on Princeton University's track and was so moved by their joy, just from competing, that my eyes welled up several times.

I also became emotional while doing one of the most difficult reports I was ever assigned. It came six months after 9/11. The piece was about widows who gave birth just days after the attacks. Their husbands never saw their newborn children. Andrea Russin of Randolph, New Jersey, was among the widows.

Andrea gave birth by caesarean section to fraternal twin girls four days after her husband, Steve, died. He was thirty-two years old and worked for the financial services firm Cantor Fitzgerald in Tower 1 at the World Trade Center.

Andrea was a thirty-four-year-old widow with three children (the couple also had an infant son) when I met her in the spring of

2002. I was amazed at her positive attitude. She told me how she met Steve in 1994 at a bar in the World Financial Center near the Twin Towers. She showed me home videos of her with Steve and their infant son, Alec. One of the videos was taken five days before the attacks, on Alec's first day of preschool. Every time Steve's image appeared, Alec ran towards the TV and shouted, "Daddy!"

That was too much for me to see without tearing up. I tried to hide my tears from Andrea because I was about to interview her. I thought if I lost my composure the interview would be more difficult for her. She was articulate, smart, and poised, especially considering the unimaginable tragedy she endured.

I had a terrible flu when I woke up on 9/11 and called in sick two hours before the planes hit the towers. As soon as I read about it online, I called the station and said I'd be there in a half hour. Like the other New York stations and most nationwide, we dropped all commercials. We went wall to wall with 9/11 coverage from that Tuesday until the following Sunday. The station put up staffers at a nearby hotel, but I didn't live far away and went home every night. I wanted to be with my family.

All the New York and New Jersey bridges and tunnels were closed by the time I arrived at the station, so I reported live on the set with any morsel of information I could find. I took a lot of calls from eyewitnesses, and we put them on the air live over the phone. For the next two months virtually every story I did was about the attacks, including many from Ground Zero on the recovery and cleanup efforts.

My clothes stunk from the rubble's fumes when I returned to the station at night. I interviewed survivors who worked in the towers, first responders, victims' loved ones and Mayor Giuliani. My heart broke for people who came up to me holding photos of their loved ones, pleading on camera for viewers to contact police if they had seen them. This happened for days after the attacks, when it was obvious that their loved ones were not alive.

After four days of nonstop 9/11 coverage, our news director told our on-air staff that we needed to report with a less morbid tone because so many people were depressed. I thought, *Really? People are depressed about the worst tragedy on American soil? You don't say.* But he had a point, and I thought there was a way to solemnly report the story without any theatrics.

One reporter took the edict too far. She did a live shot near Ground Zero about how so many New Yorkers were bringing food and water to the first responders. That was fine, a good and worthy story. However, she smiled so widely the entire time she was on camera, she almost appeared giddy. I thought her smile and tone were inappropriate. I didn't think we needed to report in a funereal tone for that type of story, but appearing happy just seemed wrong. Some viewers noticed it as well and called the station to complain.

I have seen many reporters take news managers' directives too far. I thought when in doubt about exactly what the boss means, simply ask. It's not rocket science.

On November 12, 2001, I did one of my first reports since 9/11 that was not directly about the attacks. American Airlines Flight 587 from New York's JFK Airport bound for the Dominican Republic crashed in a residential neighborhood in Belle Harbor, Queens, shortly after takeoff. All 260 people aboard the plane were killed, along with 5 people on the ground. Since this was two months after 9/11, news organizations immediately speculated on the possibility that it was an act of terrorists, and reporters swarmed the scene.

I drove straight there from my New Jersey home, over an hour away. Another one of our reporters (we'll call her "Bonnie") was already there doing live shots. She interviewed residents while I went looking for eyewitnesses. I found one who got out of his home shortly before the plane destroyed it. We had only one photographer there, and I brought the eyewitness to the live shot location. My colleague was on the air and I waited next to her. The noon newscast was almost over and I was trying to get her attention. I did not want to interrupt her, but my eyewitness had told me some compelling details off camera that I wanted him to say on camera.

I moved to my colleague's side. She ignored me. I moved inches from her. To my astonishment, she literally elbowed me out of the way so I would not be seen on camera while she was reporting. I never got on the air during that broadcast, and I was pissed.

When her live shot ended I asked her, "Why did you shove me out of the way?" She claimed she didn't realize she had done it. Even bystanders approached me afterward and said they couldn't believe what they just saw.

A photographer with my station told me later that day that the elbowing incident was the talk of the market among technical people from other stations who saw our live feed. I saw it when I got back to the station that night and was incredulous.

Months later when our news director was leaving the station, we put together a gag reel for his going-away party. Gag reels were sometimes shown when a well-liked employee was leaving. My gag started with the actual live shot of my colleague elbowing me. I had my editor put in a bit we taped behind the station. I stood at the top of a small, leafy hill. I held a microphone as though I were waiting to go on the air. I fell backwards to the ground, as if I were pushed, and rolled about twenty feet down the hill. I then looked up at the camera and, with my coat covered with leaves, held my mic up and said, "OK, Bonnie, *you* can do the live shot."

The skit got the biggest laugh when the reel was played during the party. "Bonnie" wasn't there and never mentioned it to me.

People have often asked me if I was ever punched or attacked while reporting. Besides the gypsy's bodyguard swinging the baseball bat, there were two incidents. One happened in the late '90s in Hoboken, New Jersey. Frank Sinatra's hometown had undergone gentrification and was a popular place for yuppies because it was a quick train ride to New York and less expensive. Many new restaurants and bars opened, and some longtime residents were angry about the noise that loitering patrons were making late at night.

When the bars closed, some customers urinated on residents' lawns and in businesses' parking lots. A photographer was getting a shot of a young guy peeing near a business at around 2 a.m. We made sure to keep our distance and were at such an angle that the actual peeing and the guy's face couldn't be seen. He still didn't appreciate that. He finished his business adjacent to the business, and shoved me while spitting on my face. Without thinking I shoved him back, hard. He staggered up against a concrete wall. I lost my cool. Yes, it was late and I was tired. That's no excuse. It was the only time in my career I retaliated physically. I was embarrassed and didn't show the shoving in the piece.

In the early 2000s I was preparing to do a live shot on a frigid night in midtown Manhattan. The piece was about homeless people who preferred to sleep on the street rather than in a shelter. I always was sensitive to shooting only wide shots of homeless folks and not showing their faces unless they wanted to talk. I also made sure our camera location was a good distance away.

It was about five minutes to my 10 p.m. live hit when I got hit. One of the homeless people in the group about one hundred feet in front of me threw a beer bottle and got me hard in the shin. It hurt like hell and was bleeding. It was close to airtime, so there was nothing I could do until afterwards. The cut didn't require stitches, and my shin was just black and blue and sore for a couple of days.

Any report on the homeless reminds me of the time a WWOR reporter did a live shot from a homeless shelter dressed up and wearing an expensive fur coat. She apparently didn't think about the incongruity of it. The news director later told her to dress casually from then on when reporting from a homeless shelter.

CHAPTER FORTY

Unbalanced Coverage

"The cable news channels need to change their names."

—My reaction to biased coverage

T he term "fake news" was made popular by Donald Trump during his 2015 presidential campaign. The term was reportedly first used in 2014 by a media editor for the online site Buzzfeed. The editor was researching fake online websites that claimed to be legitimate news organizations. Those sites made up news to try to sway the public. They deserved the title "fake news." But Trump brought the phrase to the forefront. I think it's one of the most overused terms in the English language.

Other than websites made up by political extremists too cowardly to use their real names or simply pushing their agendas, I don't believe there is fake news. I call it "mistake news." There are plenty of mistakes made by the mainstream media, and every reporter has biases. But "fake news" implies a story was intentionally made up. I don't buy it.

I do think the cable news channels are being disingenuous. They're not merely reporting the news; they are offering their opinions and giving commentaries. In the old days during a newscast when an opinion piece aired, it was labeled as such. Like a newspaper op-ed piece.

I think the most watched cable news networks need to be renamed. Fox News should be called "Right Wing News." CNN should be "Liberal News" and MSNBC should be re-titled "Left Wing News." What all three networks are doing, especially with their nightly shows, isn't close to objective reporting. Turn on MSNBC and you'll see the hosts and the guests bashing Trump and fellow Republicans for hours on end. Switch to Fox News and the negative Trump stories are rarely mentioned, but you'll see plenty of pieces blasting Democrats and his other critics. By comparison, I have found most local newscasts to be down the middle and fair. Many viewers disagree, based on their political beliefs.

I received calls for help from viewers who told me they believe the news media reports fake news. But when they needed help to solve their problem, they called a reporter. They apparently think some reporters are "fine people" when they need us. After I helped them, a few told me, "Well, you're not part of the fake news media." How convenient.

I do cringe about many things I see on local newscasts and in newsrooms. Some young reporters spend a lot more time on social media than reading about what's going on in their community or the world. It wouldn't kill some of them to know more about history and government. They might look and sound good, but I don't think many will get big-market jobs if they don't know at least basic current events. Some of them can tell you all about how everything works on social media, but couldn't name their city council members or county supervisors.

I don't like using "man on the street" interviews in most stories. It's ridiculous to get the public's take on an issue by interviewing three people. I think using man on the street interviews occasionally is okay. Such as asking people how they'll spend the money if they win the lottery, or on Black Friday asking what they want to buy. But I've always thought man on the street interviews are a waste of time in hard news stories. Like when you ask someone, "What do you think of the rising gas prices?" I'm still waiting for someone to answer "I love them and hope they keep rising."

I never liked doing live shots for the sake of it. Or watching others do them. As when a reporter was ordered by the news director or producer to report live from an empty auditorium or meeting room. The reporter's first sentence often was, "It's quiet here now but it was loud a few hours ago." Then kill the live shot and start the piece showing us video of the loud meeting! Some news managers think the viewer cares about a reporter being live or on tape. Viewers actually asked me if our studio anchors were doing the newscast live or on tape. They couldn't tell the difference.

I didn't like using the word "exclusive" in my stories. The viewers don't care. They don't sit at home with three or four TVs on each channel and say, "Look, Helen, Channel 4 has this story but Channel 9 missed it." Only news managers do that. A veteran reporter I worked with in New York defined "exclusive" as "the stories nobody else wants."

News consultants are the bane of many anchors and reporters. Stations pay big bucks for consultants to tell them how to do things. Many are failed former news managers who live out of town and know little about the towns in which their clients are located. They tell stations how to do stuff in a cookie-cutter, "one size fits all" fashion. They think what works in New York works in Cleveland or Tucson. News managers should trust their own judgement and experience and not have to pay outsiders to tell them what works and what doesn't.

When a local sports team is in the playoffs, some anchors and reporters become cheerleaders. I don't think there's anything wrong with rooting for the home team, but some reporters take it too far. Management at many stations seems to love it, especially when its station carries the team's games. The team's success means more games, and more games mean more revenue.

Fox 5 in New York carried the Yankees games when I worked in the city. One of its reporters wore a Yankees cap while doing live reports during the playoffs and World Series. This isn't the biggest journalistic crime ever, but I think it's unprofessional and provincial. It struck me as something you would see in a small market or on a college station. You would never see a major-market newspaper reporter wearing a team cap while working. There's an old saying, "No cheering in the press box." Fox 5 management apparently saw nothing wrong with that reporter wearing a Yankees cap on the air.

I love newspapers, and after college I might have applied at papers if I didn't get the WCBS Radio job. I'm a newspaper junkie and still love holding a hard copy in my hands. When I worked in New York I read three papers a day. I still read at least three a day now, but I confess they are all online.

Newspaper reporters have said some nice things about me, but I was criticized twice. The great columnist Jimmy Breslin did a piece in the *New York Daily News* about reporters parking in press zones in the city. The news media could buy special license plates for fifty dollars a year that permitted parking in those zones. That was a big perk since parking lots were expensive. Breslin thought it was an unfair perk and mentioned several reporters' names who parked in press zones, including mine. I thought he should have blamed the city officials who approved it, not those who parked there. We weren't breaking the law. I later found out Breslin never learned how to drive. Maybe he wrote the column because he had nothing to lose. That piece notwithstanding, I loved Breslin's work.

New York Post sports media critic Phil Mushnick didn't approve of several pieces I did on World Wrestling Entertainment stars. He wrote something to the effect of "Matthew Schwartz, usually a serious investigative reporter, has been doing fluff interviews with WWE wrestlers."

If Mushnick had called me, I would have told him that a producer wrote the pieces; I only voiced them and did a few of the interviews. However, Mushnick, even though he usually wrote repetitive and negative columns and still does, was right. Investigative reporters hurt their credibility by doing promotional pieces. The stories ran on Channel 9's Thursday-night newscasts before a WWE show. I walked into my news director's office and told him about my concerns. Thankfully, he immediately stopped having me do wrestling pieces.

CHAPTER FORTY-ONE

Mistakes, I've Made a Few

SOUND BITE:

"The report of my death is an exaggeration."

—Samuel Langhorne Clemens, American writer and humorist better known by his pen name, Mark Twain, after a newspaper printed his obituary

The worst mistake a journalist can make is to report the death of someone who is, in fact, still alive. That happened to reporters in three of the six markets in which I've worked. A .500 batting average is unheard of at most levels of baseball. In journalism, it's really, really bad.

I was working in New York in the '90s when an anchor did what's called a VO, for voice-over. The anchor's voice is heard over video, usually for fifteen or twenty seconds. One VO on our 10 o'clock newscast killed the actor Abe Vigoda. He was best known for his roles in the television sitcom *Barney Miller* and the classic films *The Godfather,* and *The Godfather Part II.* Our anchor, who did not write the story, referred to him as "the late Abe Vigoda." A colleague saw the story in a local newspaper and didn't bother to confirm it.

Taking stories from papers and websites without confirming the information is not uncommon in many television newsrooms.

The day after Abe's obituary aired a call came into the newsroom. It was Abe Vigoda.

My colleague who spoke with Vigoda told me he was good natured about it. He said, "Young lady, this is Abe Vigoda and I just want you to know I'm still very much alive." It reminded me of Twain's legendary quote.

Fortunately, I've never killed anyone, but I made my share of mistakes. The worst one I can remember happened during a live report on November 7, 1991. National Basketball Association star Ervin "Magic" Johnson announced earlier that day he had the HIV virus. The New York Knicks were playing that night and I was sent by my assignment editor to Madison Square Garden to get reactions from players for my 10 o'clock piece. I was outside the Garden standing on top of the live truck due to a large, curious crowd that usually forms in New York and elsewhere during live shots. Standing on the sidewalk in those situations often leads to trouble from someone who wants to get on TV and will do anything to be in the shot.

In my ten second lead-in to the piece, I reported, "Magic Johnson has AIDS." I knew the difference between AIDS and HIV, but misstated a very important fact. I had rushed to make deadline, but that's no excuse. I was up against the clock countless times before. My producer told me about it the next day, and I felt awful.

I remember two other times when I screwed up badly on the air (maybe my memory blocked out more mistakes). They weren't factual errors. I just came out looking bad due to being disorganized. One mistake happened during my first TV job, at WUTR in Utica. That was a good place to make mistakes because not a lot of people saw them, being one of the smallest TV markets in the country.

The people in Utica were friendly, but I couldn't stand the weather. The winters started weeks before Thanksgiving. They were cold and snowy and there were many gray days year-round. But I had to start somewhere, and WUTR hired me after a brief on-camera audition and writing test. I didn't even need to show them a tape, which was a good thing, because I didn't have one. They liked that I worked in New York. Even though it was radio and I was a gopher, it was part of CBS and in the number one market. Experienced radio guys there had told me to go into television, because it paid better and was the future of local news.

So, I called stations in the Upstate New York markets of Utica, Syracuse, and Rochester. They weren't too far from my family's New Jersey home. I told the news directors I was going to be in their towns on vacation, which was sort of true. My vacation was going to be job-hunting.

The news director at WUTR called me two days after my audition and said I was hired as a general assignment reporter. I was thrilled.

The Utica job went well considering I was a rookie and had almost no idea how to put a report together. A few months after starting I was asked to fill in as the anchor. My girlfriend at the time was visiting from New Jersey and watching the newscast from the studio. I was trying to impress her. The show started off well, but about five minutes in I turned a page in my stack of scripts and the next page was upside down. The station did not have a teleprompter, but all I had to do was turn the page right side up. Instead, I looked up at the camera, paused, and turned to the next page. It was also upside down. Now I was in a panic. I looked up again, then looked down at my scripts for what seemed like an eternity. I couldn't figure out which page was upside down and which was the correct side up. I looked up at the camera and down at my scripts at least three times. I pursed my lips, then thought it was time to regroup. I looked at the camera and said, "We'll be right back."

The director later told me that my confusion was apparent to him and he went to the break quickly. From then on when I anchored, I always checked that the scripts were right side up at least twice before the newscast started.

I worked with a cranky photographer in Utica. I think his disposition was due to him being relatively old to be working in such a small market with a small salary. When I'd arrive at work and say, "Good morning," he often replied with, "We have 300 feet of film today." That's not a lot, and it put pressure on me to do a usable stand-up on the first take (a stand-up is the reporter talking on camera during the report). The pressure helped me immeasurably. Eight years later when I started in New York, some photographers called me "First take Matt." I confess that I liked the nickname.

Another mistake I made lasted for three minutes, an entire sportscast, and it was excruciating. It was also seen by a lot more viewers than there were in Utica, because it happened in New York City.

I was filling in anchoring sports during the noon newscast on WWOR on January 28, 1986. It was an hour-long broadcast and I would come on at about 12:40 p.m. Like all newsrooms, TV monitors were on the walls, tuned to the other local stations and national cable networks. I was typing a story when I looked at the nearest monitor above my head to watch the Space Shuttle Challenger launch. Like everyone else, I was shocked when it exploded seventy-three seconds after takeoff.

I couldn't concentrate after seeing that and still needed to write more of my sports copy and review the videos I'd be voicing over. I expected the news director to drop sports and devote the entire hour to the disaster and was surprised that he didn't. He was busy planning the rest of the day's coverage of the explosion with assignment editors and producers. I was afraid to interrupt their meeting to ask if sports was being dropped. I'm sure if I had asked, it would have been canceled.

I watched more coverage of the Challenger while preparing for my sportscast. It seemed ridiculous to be writing about some game following the disaster.

My sportscast was a personal disaster. I was all over the place. My tapes and scripts were out of order. I would start a story and the highlights I'd be voicing over would be from a different game. If that happened today, it would have a ton of views on social media. I had no valid excuses for my shoddy work. But I did come away with another reminder that no matter what may be happening before going on the air, I needed to focus on my job and block out the noise. I had been able to ignore worse distractions during chaotic live shots over the years, standing in the middle of large crowds, sometimes with sirens blaring and people screaming, but the Challenger disaster scrambled my concentration.

After my horrible sportscast, I tried to console myself by thinking that probably not many people saw it because they were watching the networks live coverage of the Challenger. But I quickly thought to stop feeling sorry for myself, thinking about the astronauts and the school teacher, Christa McAuliffe, who were on board the space shuttle.

One mistake I made wasn't a quickie; it was an entire story. I was way too easy on a well-known person. Rich Rodriguez had been fired in early 2018 as head football coach at the University of Arizona amid unseemly allegations.

He was known as "Rich Rod" and he made six million dollars a year. His longtime administrative assistant, Melissa Wilhelmsen (now Melissa Melendez), accused him of sexual harassment and creating a "hostile workplace." She sued him for seven and a half million. Wilhelmsen later filed a Notice Of Claim (a precursor to a lawsuit) against the university for an additional $8.5 million, saying the school was liable for Rodriguez's alleged behavior. Wilhelmsen claimed Rodriguez sexually harassed her by brushing up against her breasts, and that he once grabbed his genitals while she was in his office. She also said she was forced to hide Rodriguez's longtime relationship with a mistress.

Rodriguez strongly denied all of Wilhelmsen's claims except the one about his extramarital affair, for which he apologized. He called the charges "extortion." He pointed out that he fully cooperated with an investigation conducted by an outside law firm and passed a polygraph test.

The law firm determined there was not enough evidence to fire Rodriguez for cause.

Nevertheless, the university fired Rodriguez *without* cause, and paid him his buyout of $6.28 million. UA's president and athletic director said they became aware of information which caused them to "be concerned with the climate and direction of the football program." They did not elaborate.

In March 2019, Rodriguez agreed to do his first TV interview, with our sports director Paul Cicala, since getting fired fourteen months earlier. The reason Rodriguez chose KVOA was simple: his daughter, Raquel, was the producer of our 4 p.m. newscast, a hardworking young woman with a good attitude.

Cicala was going to do a soft piece, a "what's Rich Rod up to now" story (he had been hired as the offensive coordinator at the University of Mississippi). I thought that the first time a guy spoke publicly about such sordid claims, it should be an investigative piece with tough questions. But I didn't want to steal anyone's story. And I like Cicala; he's a good guy, hard worker, and a friend. But at the last minute, the news director assigned the interview to me. I had been clamoring to do the interview for weeks, and told Raquel and my news director that I wanted to do it. However, I was unaware that it had been assigned to Cicala until the day before. Coach Rodriguez found out about the switch hours before the interview, when his daughter informed him. That's when I received a call from the coach's wife.

Rita Rodriguez told me she had seen my reports and knew I would ask tough questions. I told her I had to ask them and that this was a chance for Rich Rod to say what he wanted and tell his side of the story. She said okay, grudgingly. I then told the news director about Rita's call and she said I should proceed with the interview. I discussed this with Cicala and he said he understood the situation.

I felt some pressure to go soft on Rodriguez, and the interview wasn't terrible. Rodriguez got choked up and held back tears at times, especially when he said he had been excited about coaching his son and now could not. Rhett Rodriguez was UA's backup quarterback. I asked several questions about how Rodriguez learned of his firing. He said the university told him in an email, not in person or even on the phone. He said he found that "frustrating," and that "it still hurts."

But I failed to ask several tough questions. I didn't ask anything about the specific allegations because I found the guy likable. We talked football before the camera was rolling and about his new job at Ole Miss. His wife was sitting in the interview room off camera, adding to the pressure I felt. Still, I failed miserably. The guy was accused of having done some seriously wrong things and I never got into specifics with him. He might have denied everything, as he had previously, but that wasn't the point. I didn't *try* to get his answers to the ugly specifics.

You're never too old to learn, and at sixty-five years old, I was reminded not to be intimidated by outside factors. Even if they involve a colleague and a public figure you find likable.

What is probably my favorite quote ever doesn't come from a story I did, but from National Football League Hall of Fame coach Bill Parcells. Coincidentally, Parcells graduated from the same high school I did, twelve years earlier. His younger sister was in my graduating class and I knew his younger brother.

I met Parcells in the New York Giants locker room in 1986 when I was filling in reporting sports before the playoffs.

Parcells said, "You are what your record says you are."

That applies to everyone. Serial killers, elected officials, judges, salesmen, home contractors, doctors, dentists, cops, business owners, basketball players and coaches, TV news managers, and investigative reporters.

The quote says it all about how a life is lived. In the end, you hope you had a good record. You hope you made a difference in your community.

My mother did. I hope I did, too.

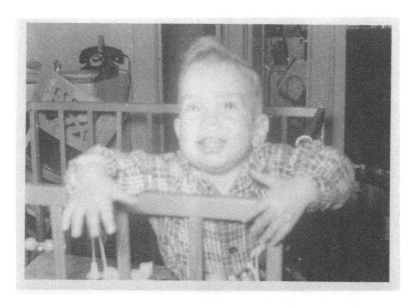

Trying to do a standup at 16 months.

My mother, Shirley Schwartz, on her 68th birthday in 1992.
She was a fighter for the less fortunate.

The promotions department told me to look tough.

With the original Colonel Sanders while working at my first TV job, Utica, New York, circa 1977.

Interviewing the serial killer David Berkowitz, aka the "Son of Sam".

I brought Berkowitz newspaper clips about his murders
but he didn't want to read them.

This trainer at Tucson Greyhound Park wasn't telling me
I'm his number one investigative reporter. The guy was later banned
for life from the since-closed track.

This salesman didn't like my questions. He was selling baby furniture and
I caught him misleading consumers into thinking he was affiliated with a
government safety council.

Anchoring in Utica, NY, 1977.
My apologies for the bad photo
quality, bad hair, and bad tie.

Outside a county jail in New Jersey around 1985 after inmates escaped.

In Tucson, 2014.

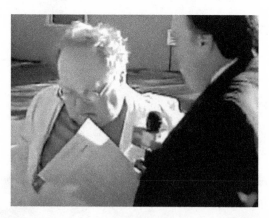

Confronting Dr. Hays about him over prescribing painkillers.

Salesmen I exposed for doing questionable things were often camera shy.

I got a lot of hugs from viewers over the years. This couple got scammed by a towing company. The woman is holding a check for $4200.

Reporting live at Dole headquarters during the 1996 New Hampshire primary.

ACKNOWLEDGMENTS

This book would not have been written while I was still working full time if I hadn't met a woman with the mellifluous name of Lala Corriere. Lala is a Tucson-based author and asked me to speak to her writers group in 2014. After she heard some of my stories, she became about the thousandth person to tell me, "You've got to write a book." I told her I had been taking notes for years and would write one when I retired. She told me to stop procrastinating, and offered this simple but sound advice: "Write a page a day." I did. Then Lala read the manuscript, twice. She believes in paying it forward, and she did with me. Thank you, "Red," for your advice, your time, and for pushing a reluctant author.

There's an old saying that you're lucky to have one great friend. I have several. Alan Dopf has been like a brother to me since the fourth grade. Nearly sixty years later our friendship endures.

Jim Randle taught me how to put a news report together. We met in 1977 when I joined him at WUTR-TV in Utica. Jim let me live with him for a while until I found an apartment. Jim had a marvelous broadcasting career at Voice of America and I'm grateful we've kept in touch.

Jim Bailey showed me that not only could competitors be friends, they could be roommates. Jim and I hung out when we were wild, young, and single in Richmond, Virginia. We roomed together after we met at the ABC affiliate, and remained roommates after the NBC station "stole" me. Jim had a wonderful TV news career. He's also the only guy I fixed up on a date. Now, Jim and Jackie have been married for almost forty years. Thanks to both of you for your southern hospitality, your friendship, and kindness.

My team of beta readers made excellent suggestions. They include Leslie Gilpatrick and two smart TV news producers and former New York colleagues, Allen Levine and Michael Horowicz.

I appreciate the time three former colleagues took to send me scripts. Thank you, Allison Gilbert in New York and Matt McGlashen and Vicky Benchimol in Tampa.

Thanks to a First Amendment wizard, attorney Dan Barr of Perkins Coie LLP, for reviewing portions of the book.

Photographers are the unsung heroes of the news business. They carry heavy equipment, deal with dangerous situations, bad weather, and difficult reporters. I thank every one of the hundreds of photogs I worked with, and all the editors who put my stories together.

I deeply appreciate the faith that John Koehler, president and publisher of Koehler Books, had in a first-time author. Kudos to Joe Coccaro, Koehler's vice president and executive editor, for his guidance.

Thanks to a brilliant web designer named Mike Erickson, owner of uExclusive. Without him, this technologically challenged reporter would still be trying to set up my website, MatthewSchwartzBook.com.

Thanks to my partner, Susan, for letting me lock myself into my home office on nights and weekends while writing this book, and for her tremendous support in every way.

I am incredibly proud of my children, Michael, Jason, and Jessica, especially for how kind-hearted and caring they are. I am lucky to have two wonderful brothers, Adam, a great writer who suggested the book's title, and David, who has always been there for me and could be elected mayor of our hometown of River Edge, if he chose to run.

Writing a book was a dream of mine and the first of three items on my bucket list. Next up, learning to play piano and trying to act in community theater.

Or, because this has been such a blast, maybe I'll write another book first.

ABOUT THE AUTHOR

Matthew Schwartz has told approximately 10,000 stories on television stations across the country for four decades. He has won more than 200 awards, including four New York Emmys and four regional Edward R. Murrow Awards for Investigative Reporting.

Some of Matthew's most memorable stories include an interview with the "Son of Sam" serial killer David Berkowitz; the trials of mobster John Gotti; reports on the 9/11 attacks from Ground Zero; the crash two months later of American Airlines Flight 587 in Queens, NY; the bombing of Pam Am flight 103 over Lockerbie, Scotland; and hundreds of reports on corruption, fraud, and government waste.

CPSIA information can be obtained
at www.ICGtesting.com
Printed in the USA
BVHW030529250220
573214BV00003B/8

9 781646 630738